A TRIBUTE TO TEACHERS

A
TRIBUTE
TO
TEACHERS

Wit and Wisdom,
Information and Inspiration About
Those Who Change Our Lives

RICHARD LEDERER

Marion Street Press

Portland, Oregon

to Deedy—mother, teacher, and eternal learner

Acknowledgments

I thank Dan Moulthrop, Bill Guy, and Frank Caso for providing some of the data in this treasury. I'm also grateful to Taylor Mali, William Hiss, Joseph J. Mazzella, and Arthur Benjamin for granting me permission to reprint their contributions. A version of the first half of "Excuses, Excuses" appears in my *Anguished English* (Gibbs Smith 2006).

I have striven mightily to track down the source of every item in this book that isn't of my own making. To those creators whom I have not been able to identify, I hope you are pleased that your luminous contributions gleam, albeit anonymously, from these pages.

Published by Marion Street Press
4207 S.E. Woodstock Blvd. # 168
Portland, OR 97206-6267
USA
http://www.marionstreetpress.com/

Orders and review copies: 800-888-4741

Printed in the United States of America
ISBN 978-1-936863-02-0

Back cover photo by Kim Treffinger

Library of Congress Cataloging-in-Publication Data

Lederer, Richard, 1938-
   A tribute to teachers : wit and wisdom, information and inspiration about those who change our lives / Richard Lederer.
      p. cm.
   ISBN 978-1-936863-02-0 (pbk.)
   1. Teachers--Conduct of life. 2. Teachers--Humor. 3. Teachers--Anecdotes.
I. Title.
   LB1775.L373 2011
   371.1--dc23
                                        2011029953

Table of Contents

Introduction / *vii*

1. The Private Lives of Real Teachers / 1
2. A Gallery of Great Teachers / 4
3. Why Teachers Matter / 9
4. A Teacher's Salary / 13
5. What Teachers Make / 17
6. Life According to Student Bloopers / 19
7. Sunday School Bloopers / 23
8. Excuses, Excuses / 26
9. A Teacher's Dictionary / 29
10. The Creation of Teachers / 32
11. A Teacher's Tale / 35
12. Educated Bumper Snickers / 38
13. Lists Every Teacher Should Know / 40
14. Figures of Teach / 43
15. Students Say the Darnedest Things / 46
16. Jumping to Confusions / 50
17. The School Family / 52
18. The Classroom Lives of Real Teachers / 56
19. Teachers in Literature / 58
20. Teacher Flicks / 60
21. Famous School Reports—Characters / 64
22. Famous Teacher Reports—People / 67
23. Teachers' Advice to Students / 70
24. Classy Puns / 74
25. Have You Heard? / 77
26. Why I Flunked Out of High School / 80
27. Animal Cracker Uppers / 82
28. A Teacher's Covenant / 85
29. Short Takes / 87

30. Schoolishness / 90

31. A Remarkable School / 94

32. Language Arts / 96

33. Building Better Vocabularies / 99

34. Under a Spell / 101

35. Proverbial Wisdom / 105

36. Science Friction / 107

37. Doing the Numbers / 110

38. Hysterical History / 114

39. Lost in Translation / 117

40. More Teacher Tales / 119

41. A Teacher's Night Before Christmas / 122

42. A Teacher's Garden of Verses / 124

43. Education Quotations / 127

44. A Teacher's Legacy / 131

Introduction

*What nobler employment, or more valuable to the state,
than the person who instructs the rising generation.*
–MARCUS TULLIUS CICERO

*What office is there which involves more responsibility,
which requires more qualifications,
and which ought, therefore, to be more honorable, than that of teaching?*
–HARRIET MARTINEAU

A teacher affects eternity. No one can tell where his influence stops.
–HENRY ADAMS

*Teaching is the only profession where you can run into someone
who is forty-five and they will call you by your name
and tell you something you did many years ago that changed their life.*
–STEVE LILLY

During the presidency of Dwight David Eisenhower, James Michener, author of *Hawaii, The Source,* and other mega-sellers, was invited to a celebrity dinner at the White House. In a letter Michener declined to attend: "Dear Mr. President: I received your invitation three days after I had agreed to speak a few words at a dinner honoring the wonderful high school teacher who taught me how to write. I know you will not miss me at your dinner, but she might at hers."

A week later, Michener received a handwritten reply from the understanding Ike: "In his lifetime a man lives under fifteen or sixteen presidents, but a really fine teacher comes into his life but rarely. Go and speak at your teacher's dinner."

Teaching is the highest calling. Parents entrust their most precious treasures to teachers. Almost everybody who is anybody was taught to be somebody by a teacher. Teaching is the profession that teaches all the other professions.

America is a nation of teachers: The Bureau of Labor Statistics, in their 2008–2009 *Occupational Outlook Handbook*, counts 6,085,000 teachers in the United States. This includes 3,954,000 pre-kindergarten- to twelfth-grade teachers, 459,000 special education teachers, and 1,672,000 postsecondary professors and instructors.

Teachers are not only a populous group across our land. They change the lives of our young people. In *What the Dog Saw*, Malcolm Gladwell states, "Teacher effects dwarf school effects: your child is actually better off in a bad school with an excellent teacher than in an excellent school with a bad teacher." Study after study shows that great teaching is the most important booster of student achievement—of larger consequence than class size, money spent, the school building, and quality of textbooks.

One of my favorite newspaper corrections reads: "It was incorrectly reported last Friday that today is T-shirt Appreciation Week. It is actually Teacher Appreciation Week." In 1985, the National Education Association and National Parent Teacher Association set aside the first full week in May as a time to honor teachers and show respect for their profession. In fact, every day should be devoted to teacher appreciation and made a time to recognize members of the most unheralded, labor-intensive, multitasking, exhausting, income-challenged, and rewarding of all professions.

What you are reading is a Teacher Appreciation Book. I wrote it because I believe that an apple lasts a short time in the hands of a teacher, but a bit of wisdom lasts a lifetime in the mind and heart of a student.

I believe that teachers deserve the nice things people say about them. Having been an English teacher (an inmate in the House of Correction) for twenty-eight years, I'm biased of course. To George Bernard Shaw's mean sneer, "He who can, does. He who cannot, teaches," I would oppose Lee Iacocca's "In a truly rational world, the best of us would be teachers, and the rest of us would do something else."

Or I would quote Shaw himself: "To me the sole hope of human salvation lies in teaching."

Blessed be the teachers. Harmonies of scholars, mentors, counselors, coaches, cheerleaders, traffic controllers, judges, sculptors, artists, interior decorators, janitors, nurses, baby-sitters, comedians, clowns, tightrope walkers, acrobats, and jugglers, they march in the company of secular saints. May their tribe increase and thrive.

Richard Lederer
San Diego, California
richard.lederer@pobox.com
www.verbivore.com

The Private Lives of Real Teachers

My wife is a teacher; it's really weird to live with a teacher.
I'd be on the phone, doodling on a piece of paper,
leave the house, come back in two hours,
and that same piece of paper is now on the refrigerator
with the words "Great work!" and a big smiley face on it.
–LEW SCHNEIDER

Here's a true story: Beth, a high school English teacher in Maine, lived with her friend Sam, an intelligent golden retriever. One day, Beth's mother was riding in the back seat of the car with Sam, who insisted on leaning on Mother. Mother told Sam to "lay down and behave." No action. Mother repeated, "Lay down, Sam." Still no response.

Then Beth commanded, "*Lie* down, Sam," and down the dog went. He was, after all, the companion of an English teacher.

Beth is a real teacher, and real teachers are rare and astonishing people:

Real teachers give themselves away in public because of the dry erase pen marker smudges all over their hands. Real teachers can't walk past a crowd of people without snapping their fingers, straightening up the line, and correcting behavior. Real teachers ask quiet people at parties if they have anything to share with the group. When anyone leaves the party, real teachers ask them if they have forgotten their hats, scarves, and mittens. Real teachers always have a tissue in hand in case somebody sneezes. When real teachers empty their pockets at night, they find two used hall passes, one unused bus pass, a pencil stub, and no money.

Real teachers' relatives refuse to attend their parties if "it's going to be mostly teachers" because they all talk shop. Real teachers amaze and annoy their friends by correcting their grammar. Real teachers move their dinner partner's glass away from the edge of the table. Real teachers refer to happy hour as "snack time."

Real teachers are irritated by adults who chew gum in public, and they hand pieces of paper to their friends and make them spit out their gum in front of them. Real teachers declare "no cuts" when a shopper squeezes ahead of them in a checkout line. Real teachers ask if anyone needs to go to the bathroom as they enter a theater with a group of friends. In a theater, real teachers often turn around and shush the people behind them. Real teachers send other adults to detention when they use bad language—and they go! Real teachers' voices are permanently set on high volume from attempting to be heard over students' voices day after day. Any loud noise at home causes them to impulsively flick the light switch off and on.

Real teachers say, "I like the way you did that!" to the mechanic who successfully repairs their car. They ask, "Are you sure you did your best?" to the mechanic who fails to repair their car satisfactorily. Real teachers say everything twice. Real teachers say everything twice.

Real teachers wear fuzzy slippers with little animal faces on them. At least one item of their jewelry lights up. Real teachers have at least a dozen colorful sweaters and sweatshirts for each of the holidays, including Flag Day. Real teachers are among the nation's biggest buyers of pipe cleaners. Their neighbors drop off empty coffee cans, margarine cups, L'eggs eggs, milk bottle cartons, scraps of material, and old newspapers at their home.

Real teachers have no social life between August and June. Real teachers want to slap upside the head anybody who says, "Must be nice to work from only 8:00 AM to 3:00 PM and have summers off." While everyone else at the beach is catching up on the latest novels, real teachers are cutting out little oak tag people for their September bulletin boards. Real teachers make little turkey name tags for everyone at their family's Thanksgiving dinner.

So . . .

- If you sing "The Alphabet Song" to yourself as you look up a number in the telephone book;
- If you fold your spouse's fingers over the coins as you hand him or her the money at a soda machine;
- If your own children must raise their hand to capture your attention;
- If your refrigerator door looks like a military command center because it is covered with notes, calendars, coupons, phone numbers, and a thousand other things;
- If one of the drawers in your kitchen is full of pencils, pens, crayons, markers, erasers, glue, and the like;
- If you stop at the curb to pick up discarded old shelves, bookcases, file cabinets, or magazine racks;

    . . . then, even if you don't work at a school, you are a real teacher.

A Gallery of Great Teachers

I have come to believe that a great teacher is a great artist,
and there are as few as there are any other great artists.
Teaching might even be the greatest of the arts
since the medium is the human mind and spirit.
–JOHN STEINBECK

Better than a thousand days of diligent study
is one day with a great teacher.
–CHINESE PROVERB

The mediocre teacher tells. The good teacher explains.
The superior teacher demonstrates. The great teacher inspires.
–WILLIAM ARTHUR WARD

A master can tell you what he expects of you.
A teacher, though, awakens your own expectations.
–PATRICIA NEAL

Enlightening the Night

The Chinese philosopher Confucius (551–479 B.C.) may have been the world's first advocate of public school open to all. "Ignorance is the night of the mind, but a night without moon or stars," Confucius said. Before he became founder of the religion Confucianism, he gathered a large number of students around him and instructed them in history, poetry, ritual, and music. He never refused a sincere student "even if he came to me on foot, with nothing more to offer as tuition than a package of dried meat."

"In education, there should be no class distinctions," he wrote. "Even a peasant boy can become a man of intellect and principle."

A Mighty Line of Teachers

The Greek philosopher Socrates (469–399 B.C.) believed that everyone possessed true knowledge. He broke with earlier philosophical traditions and laid the foundations for the development of both ethics and logic. His Socratic method of teaching was to ask probing questions that would bring this preexisting knowledge to consciousness. Refusing to bow to tyranny and irrationality, Socrates was charged with corrupting the young people of Athens and sentenced to death by drinking hemlock.

Socrates' most famous pupil was Plato, whose most famous student was Aristotle. And Aristotle's most famous pupil was . . .

A Great Student

In 343 B.C., when Alexander the Great was thirteen years old, he became a pupil of the philosopher Aristotle of Stagira (384–322 B.C.). "I am indebted to my father for living, but to my teacher for living well," wrote the pupil.

Aristotle inspired Alexander to love literature, history, culture, sports, and physical fitness. Such teaching influenced Alexander to bring the Greek Way to the many countries that he conquered. "Teachers, who educate children, deserve more honor than parents, who merely gave them birth; for the latter provided mere life, while the former ensure a good life," wrote the teacher. "Those that know, do. Those that understand, teach."

The Name Rings a Bell

Traveling ahead from one Alexander to another: Alexander Graham Bell (1847–1922) did not think of himself primarily as the inventor of the telephone. In fact, he saw the telephone as an intrusion on his privacy and refused to have one installed in his study.

Bell saw himself, first and foremost, as a teacher of the deaf. As a boy, he had forged a powerful bond with his mother, who was hearing impaired. As a teacher, Bell was devoted to helping deaf people speak so that they could take part in the speaking world rather than be isolated. To do this, he opened a school in Boston for teachers of the deaf, and he sought to make sound accessible in new ways.

"Before anything else, preparation is the key to success," Bell explained. His uncommon success in achieving this goal led to his inventing the telephone. Upon Bell's death in 1922, all telephones throughout the United States "stilled their ringing for a silent minute in tribute to the man whose yearning to communicate made them possible."

The Miracle Worker

Most of us cannot remember learning our first word, but Helen Keller (1880–1968) recalled that event in her life with a flashing vividness. She remembered because she was deaf, mute, and blind from the age of nineteen months and did not learn her first word until she was seven.

When Helen was six, an extraordinary teacher named Anne Sullivan (1866–1936) entered her life. Anne was poor, ill, and nearly blind herself, but she possessed a tenacious vitality that was to force her pupil's unwilling mind from the dark, silent prison in which it lived: "Before my teacher came to me, I lived in a world that was a no-world. I cannot hope to describe adequately that unconscious yet conscious time of nothingness. I did not know that I knew aught, or that I lived or acted or desired."

In *The Miracle Worker*, playwright William Gibson shows us what happened when Anne Sullivan first met Helen's mother:

> MRS. KELLER: What will you teach her first?
>
> ANNE: First, last, and in between, language.
>
> MRS. KELLER: Language.
>
> ANNE: Language is to the mind more than light is to the eye.

The miracle that Anne Sullivan worked was to give Helen Keller language. Day after day, month after month, the teacher spelled words into Helen's hand. Finally, when Helen was seven years old and working with her teacher in the presence of water, she spoke her first word. Years later she described that moment in *The Story of My Life* (1902): "Somehow the mystery of language was revealed to me. I knew then that "w-a-t-e-r" meant that wonderful cool something that was flowing over my hand. That living word awakened my soul, gave it light, hope, joy, set it free! . . . I left the well-house eager to learn. Everything had a name, and each name gave birth to a new thought." Anne Sullivan described the moment this way: "My heart is singing for joy this morning! A miracle has happened! The light of understanding has shone upon my little pupil's mind, and behold, all things are changed!"

Not only did Helen Keller learn to speak, write, and understand the English language, she graduated *cum laude* from Radcliffe College and went on to become a distinguished lecturer and writer. But perhaps the most poignant moment in her life came when, at the age of nine, she was able to say to her teacher, Anne Sullivan: "I am not dumb now."

A Path to Self Discovery

Maria Montessori (1870–1952) was a visionary. In 1896, she became the first female physician in Italy. A decade later, she gave up her practice and her university chair in Anthropology to teach a group of sixty young children of working parents in the San Lorenzo district of Rome. There she developed what ultimately became the Montessori method of education, built on her scientific observations of these children's almost effortless ability to absorb knowledge from their surroundings, as well as their tireless interest in manipulating materials.

She wrote, "Don't tell them how to do it. Show them how to do it, and don't say a word. If you tell them, they'll watch your lips move. If you show them, they'll want to do it themselves" and "The greatest sign of success for a teacher . . . is to be able to say, 'The children are working as if I did not exist.'"

Dr. Montessori's simple but profound insight was that, in the right environment, children teach themselves. "I did not invent a method of education," she wrote. "I simply gave some little children a chance to live."

Here is a selection of other great teachers throughout history. Many of them spent time in the classroom, with or without walls. All have powerfully advanced humankind and truly affected eternity:

Moses (circa 1391–1271 B.C.)	Samuel Johnson (1709–1784)
Pythagoras (circa 576–495 B.C.)	Noah Webster (1758–1843)
Euclid (323–283 B.C.)	Henry David Thoreau (1817–1862)
Jesus Christ (circa 0–A.D. 33)	Booker T. Washington (1856–1915)
Paul of Tarsus (circa 5–circa 67)	W.E.B. Dubois (1868–1963)
Marcus Aurelius (121–180)	Mahatma Gandhi (1869–1948)
Muhammad (570–632)	Albert Einstein (1879–1955)
Erasmus (1469–1536)	Martin Luther King, Jr. (1929–1968)
Galileo Galilei (1564–1642)	Jaime Escalante (1930–2010)
Isaac Newton (1643–1727)	Stephen Hawking (1948–)

Why Teachers Matter

If a man empties his purse into his mind,
no one can take it away from him.
An investment of knowledge always pays the best interest.
–BENJAMIN FRANKLIN

Liberty cannot be preserved without
a general knowledge among the people.
–JOHN ADAMS

We cannot always build the future for our youth,
but we can build our youth for the future.
–FRANKLIN D. ROOSEVELT

The classroom, not the trench,
is the frontier of freedom now and forever more.
–LYNDON JOHNSON

Education is the mother of leadership.–WENDELL L. WILKIE

Education is a better safeguard of liberty than a standing army.
–EDWARD EVERETT

Knowledge is the most democratic source of power.
–ALVIN TOFFLER

Only the educated are free.–EPICECTUS

The secret of freedom lies in educating people,
whereas the secret of tyranny is in keeping them ignorant.
–MAXIMILIEN ROBESPIERRE

Education is our passport to the future,
for tomorrow belongs to the people who prepare for it today.
–MALCOLM X

If you think education is expensive, try ignorance.–DEREK BOK

In the first major address of his presidency, Barack Obama said: "In a global economy where the most valuable skill you can sell is your knowledge, a good education is no longer just a pathway to opportunity—it is a prerequisite. . . .

"So tonight I ask every American to commit to at least one year or more of higher education or career training. . . . Dropping out of high school is no longer an option. It's not just quitting on yourself, it's quitting on your country—and this country needs and values the talents of every American."

• A young scholar once wrote, "The amount of education you have determines your loot in life." The student meant to write *lot*, but *loot* works, too. For example, four out of five millionaires are college graduates. Education does indeed determine one's loot, as demonstrated by these estimated lifetime earnings for American workers:

high school dropouts	$1 million
high school graduates	$1.2 million
Bachelor's degree holders	$2.1 million
Master's degree holders	$2.5 million
PhD holders	$3.4 million
professional degree holders	$4.4 million

The figures are clear: In 2008, high school dropouts garnered median earnings of $426 per week, compared with $757 for high school graduates and $1,072 for college graduates.

In 2009, in Falls Church, Virginia, 69.5% of all residents age twenty-five or higher earned a bachelor's degree, the highest percentage of any county or independent city equivalent to a county in the United States. Not surprisingly, the median income in Falls Church City that year was $113,313, the highest in the nation. A worker who completes a college degree earns 1.75 times the income of a worker who doesn't. Happily, 62% of all high school graduates receive at least some advanced schooling.

• Even bad times testify to the value of education. During the 2008–2009 Recession and its painful aftermath, the national jobless rate hovered around 10%. Here's a closer look at that joblessness correlated with education:

high school dropouts	*15.3%*
high school graduates	*10.3%*
college attendees	*9%*
college graduates	*4.6%*

During the Recession, high school dropouts on average lost 16% of their hourly wages, while men with postgraduate degrees added 26%.

• Two-thirds of students who cannot read proficiently by the end of the fourth grade will end up in jail or on welfare. The fourth grade is the watershed year. The average prisoner has reached the tenth grade.

• Healthy doses of education help protect the brain and keep it fit. "Even with dementia," contends Michael Kabat, a neuropsychologist at Scripps Memorial Hospital in La Jolla, California, "people with more education tend to develop it later. Nobody is exactly sure why, but what we see is that having a higher level of intellectual stimulation can have long-term benefits as you grow older."

• Worldwide the pattern has become clear that child mortality declines in proportion to the years of education that women experience. Educated women, it appears, make better choices about hygiene, nutrition, immunization, and contraception. According to a study by the Institute for Health, Metrics, and Evaluation, education accounts for 51% of the decline in global child mortality, the most significant influence by far.

- In the United States, about 25% of all people are directly involved in schools as students, teachers, or professors.

- We are a nation of students: 73.2 million United States residents are enrolled in schools—from nursery schools to colleges and trade schools. On any given weekday morning, something like 50 million Americans, about a sixth of our total population, will be sitting under the roof of a public school.

- In 1900, only 10% of American adolescents, ages fourteen to seventeen, were enrolled in high school, only 8% earned high school diplomas, and only about 2% of Americans, ages eighteen to twenty-four, attended college. By the end of the twentieth century those figures increased to 85% and 60%.

- American students spend about 20% of their waking time in school, and 59% of students, ages six to seventeen, participate in at least one of three extracurricular activities—sports, clubs, or lessons.

- Americans are devoting more years to pursuing an education than ever before: Between 1945 and 1975 the U.S. population grew 54%, yet the number of students enrolled in higher education rose more than sixfold, and the number of earned degrees grew more than tenfold. In 2010, 41% of eighteen- to twenty-four-year-olds were enrolled in college, an all-time high.

- Education matters for teachers, too: Judging from the highest degrees earned, our teachers are becoming increasingly qualified. Here are the percentages of highest degrees held by elementary through high school teachers in 1961 compared with 2001:

	1961	*2001*
less than Bachelor's	15	0
Bachelor's	62	43
Master's or six years	23	56
Doctor's	0	1

A Teacher's Salary

*Faculty: the people who get what's left
after the football coach receives his salary.*
–HENNY YOUNGMAN

*A toy company is releasing a Teacher Barbie.
Apparently, it's like Malibu Barbie, only she can't afford the Corvette.*
–STEPHANIE MILLER

*Therefore for the love of God appoint teachers and schoolmasters,
you that have the charge of youth,
and give the teachers stipends worthy of their pains.*
–BISHOP HUGH LATIMER

*A hundred years from now, it will not matter what my bank account was,
the sort of house I lived in, or the kind of car I drove.
But the world may be different because I was important
in the life of a child.*
–KATHY DAVIS

*Modern cynics and skeptics see no harm in paying those
to whom they entrust the minds of their children a smaller wage than is paid
to those to whom they entrust the care of their plumbing.*
–JOHN F. KENNEDY

In *Not Another Apple for the Teacher*, authors Erin Barrett and Jack Mingo explain, "Giving an apple to the teacher as a symbolic gesture came from a time when American teachers were often paid in farm goods by cash-poor townspeople. It wasn't easy to be a teacher—many had to take after-hour jobs as choir leaders, gravedig-gers, or bartenders in order to earn a decent living."

Sound familiar?

Real teachers let their life partners know that they won't be the primary breadwinner in their marriage. Real teachers drive rust bucket cars they're still trying to pay off and for which they can bare-ly afford the insurance. Real teachers don't wear the latest fashions, unless they got them at half price at a discount store. Real teachers have vacation time but no money to travel. Real teachers get paid to work six hours a day but actually work eight or more. Real teachers spend their summers as waiters, temps, camp counselors, and the like. When real teachers get their first paycheck in September, they are reminded that teaching is a job, not just what they love to do.

The majority of teachers get into the profession of educating oth-er people's children because they want to work with young people. They get out of it for other reasons. More than a third leave because of the low pay. As Sarah Vowell observes, "If American citizens truly believe in building a world-class public education system, we might consider paying our teachers more than third-world wages."

Teachers change the world one child at a time, yet they are sorely unappreciated. Recent surveys have shown that:

- Public school teachers work an average of ten hours per week beyond the hours stipulated in their contracts. In reality, the av-erage teacher works a fifty-hour week, including uncompensated school-related activities such as grading papers, club advising, bus duties, phone calls to students' homes, and supervision of evening events.

- The average salary for an American public school teacher in 2007–2008 was $52,308, ranging from California ($64,424) at the high end to South Dakota ($36,674) at the low end.

- The average one-year increase in public school teacher salaries is 3.1 percent, while the Consumer Price Index increases at a rate of 4.3 percent. Thus, the standard of living for teachers is constantly eroded by inflation.

- Low salary is the number one cause of new teachers leaving edu-cation, on average, after five years. Up to one-third of new teach-ers drop out within their first three years on the job. More than half of all teachers do not reach their retirement age as teachers. They have left the profession.

- Low pay contributes to gender imbalance. More than three quarters (75.5%) of public school teachers are female, and the percentage of men in classrooms has been shrinking for decades.

- In U.S. public school systems, 71% of teachers purchase books and supplies with their own money—on average, $468 each year—to make their classrooms better places and school a better experience for their students.

- Sixty-three percent of public school teachers buy food each month for their hungry students.

- In order to maintain their credentials or to move up on the salary scale, an average of 23% of teachers attend summer classes, often without recompense.

- As many as 42% of teachers work in summer schools and/or second jobs during the school year. Some tend bar or wait tables, some work in retail, some become handymen, housepainters, or landscapers. The author of this book spent many summers as an athletic director at a camp and as a window man dispensing hamburgers, french fries, desserts, and soft drinks. Then there are those teachers who take on summer school assignments, which the author did for seventeen straight summers. Hey, you have to find ways to support your teaching habit—and the straight salary can't do that.

Heavenly Admission

A young man died and went to Heaven, where he was the third person in line at the Pearly Gates.

St. Peter was taking a break, and an angel was admitting the newly arrived into Heaven. Trying to get a little stricter with the admission policies, the angel said they each had to state their former occupations and yearly salaries.

The first man in line said, "I was an actor and I earned $1 million last year." The angel ushered him in.

The woman behind him said, "I earned $350,000 last year as an attorney." The angel thought about it for a moment, then ushered her in as well.

The young man moved up to the gates. "I earned $28,000 last year . . . ," he began.

"Oh," the angel interrupted, "and what subject did you teach?"

Fed Up

I'm fed up with teachers and their hefty salary guides. What we need here is a little perspective.

If I had my way, I'd pay these teachers myself. I'd pay them baby-sitting wages. That's right: Instead of paying these outrageous taxes, I'd give them $3 an hour out of my own pocket. And I'm only paying them for five hours, not coffee breaks or lunch.

That would be $15 a day. Each parent should pay $15 a day for these teachers to babysit their child. Even if they have more than one child, it's still a lot cheaper than private day care.

Now, how many children do they teach every day—maybe twenty? That's $15 x 20 = $300 a day. But remember, they only work 180 days a year! I'm not going to pay them for all those vacations! $300 x 180 = $54,000. (Just a minute, I think my calculator needs batteries.)

Now, I know what you teachers will say: What about those who have ten years' experience and a master's degree? Well, maybe (to be fair) they could get the minimum wage, and instead of just babysitting, they could read the kids a story. We could round that off to about $5 an hour, times five hours, times twenty children. That's $500 a day times 180 days. That's $90,000 . . . HUH?

What Teachers Make

A good teacher is a pearl beyond measure.–CHARLES MURRAY

When love and skill work together, expect a masterpiece.
–JOHN RUSKIN

Kind words can be short and easy to speak, but their echoes are endless.
–MOTHER TERESA

What Teachers Make

He says the problem with teachers is
What's a kid going to learn
from someone who decided his best option in life
was to become a teacher?
He reminds the other dinner guests that it's true
what they say about teachers:
Those who can, do; those who can't, teach.
I decide to bite my tongue instead of his
and resist the temptation to remind the dinner guests
that it's also true what they say about lawyers.
Because we're eating, after all, and this is polite conversation.
I mean, you're a teacher, Taylor.
Be honest. What do you make?
And I wish he hadn't done that—
asked me to be honest—
because, you see, I have this policy
about honesty and bullies:
if you ask for it, then I have to let you have it.
You want to know what I make?
I make kids work harder than they ever thought they could.

I can make a C+ feel like a Congressional Medal of Honor
and an A- feel like a slap in the face.
How dare you waste my time
with anything less than your very best.
I make kids sit through 40 minutes of study hall
in absolute silence. *No, you may not work in groups.*
No, you may not ask a question.
Why won't I let you go to the bathroom?
Because you're bored.
And you don't really have to go to the bathroom, do you?
I make parents tremble in fear when I call home:
Hi. This is Mr. Mali. I hope I haven't called at a bad time,
I just wanted to talk to you about something your son said today.
To the biggest bully in the grade, he said,
"Leave the kid alone. I still cry sometimes, don't you?
It's no big deal."
And that was the noblest act of courage I have ever seen.

I make parents see their children for who they are
and what they can be.
You want to know what I make?
I make kids wonder,
I make them question.
I make them criticize.
I make them apologize and mean it.
I make them write.
I make them read, read, read.
I make them spell *definitely beautiful, definitely beautiful,*
     definitely beautiful
over and over and over again until they will never misspell
either one of those words again.
I make them show all their work in math
and hide it on their final drafts in English.
I make them understand that if you've got *this,*
then you follow *this,*
and if someone ever tries to judge you
by what you make, you give them *this.*
Here, let me break it down for you, so you know what I say is true:
Teachers? Teachers make a difference! Now what about you?

                                            —Taylor Mali

Life According to
Student Bloopers

Socrates was a famous Greek teacher
who went around giving people advice. They killed him.
–from a STUDENT ESSAY

One of the fringe benefits of being a teacher is discovering the occasional gem of a student blooper that gleams out from an essay or test paper. The original classroom blunder probably dates back to the day that some innocent pupil first touched quill to parchment. Ever since, students have demonstrated a remarkable facility for mixing up similar-sounding words or reinventing the simplest of facts.

The following student fluffs and flubs, goofs and gaffes, blunders, boo-boos, botches, and bloopers are authentic, genuine, certified, and unretouched. Each is worthy of a Pullet Surprise.

Top 10 History Bloopers
1. The inhabitants of ancient Egypt were called mummies, and they all wrote in hydraulics.
2. The Greeks were a highly sculptured people, and without them we wouldn't have history. The Greeks invented myths. A myth is a female moth.
3. Julius Caesar extinguished himself on the battlefields of Gaul. When the Ides of March murdered him, he expired with the words "Eat you, Brutus!"
4. William Tell shot an arrow through an apple while standing on his son's head.

5. During the Middle Ages everyone was middle aged. Life during the Middle Ages was especially difficult for the pheasants.
6. Columbus discovered America while cursing about the Atlantic on the Nina, the Pinta Colada, and the Santa Fe.
7. Sir Francis Drake circumcised the world with a hundred-foot clipper.
8. The Declaration of Independence was founded by four fathers.
9. Abraham Lincoln wrote the Gettysburg Address while traveling from Washington to Gettysburg on the back of an envelope.
10. The First World War was caused by the assignation of the Arch-Duck by an anahist. In the Second World War, Franklin Roosevelt put a stop to Hitler, who committed suicide in his bunk.

Top 10 Science Bloopers
1. Our new teacher told us all about fossils. Before she came to our class, I didn't know what a fossil looked like.
2. Scientists are hypothetical people.
3. A molecule can't be seen by the naked observer.
4. The equator is an imaginary lion that runs around the world forever.
5. Heredity means that if your grandfather didn't have any children, then your father probably wouldn't have any, and neither would you probably.
6. Genetics explains why you look like your father and if you don't, why you should.
7. Elephants eat roots, leaves, grasses, and sometimes bark.
8. The tides are a fight between the Earth and the Moon. All water tends to flow towards the moon, because there is no water on the moon, and Nature abhors a vacuum. I forget where the sun joins in this fight.
9. A planet is a body of earth surrounded by sky.
10. Sharks are ugly and mean and have big teeth, just like Emily Richardson. She's not my friend any more.

Top 10 Music Bloopers
1. Most authorities agree that music of antiquity was written long ago.
2. An opera is a song of bigly size.
3. I know what a sextet is but I had rather not say.
4. The principle singer of the nineteenth-century opera was called pre-Madonna.

5. Contralto is a low sort of music that only ladies sing.
6. All female parts were sung by castrati. We don't know exactly what they sounded like because there are no known descendants.
7. My favorite composer was Opus. Agnes Dei was a woman composer famous for her church music.
8. Johann Sebastian Bach wrote a great many music compositions and had a large number of children. In between he practiced on an old spinster which he kept up in his attic.
9. Ludwig van Beethoven wrote music even though he was deaf. He was so deaf he wrote loud music.
10. Aaron Copland is one of our most famous contemporary composers. It is unusual to be contemporary. Most composers do not live until they are dead.

Top 10 Literature Bloopers

1. One myth says that the mother of Achilles dipped him in the River Stynx until he became intolerable.
2. Achilles appears in *The Iliad*, by Homer. Homer also wrote *The Oddity*, in which Penelope is the last hardship that Odysseus endures on his journey.
3. The greatest writer of the Renaissance was William J. Shakespeare. Shakespeare was born in the year 1564, supposedly on his birthday. His father was Mr. Shakespeare, and his mother was Mrs. Shakespeare. He wrote during the era in which he lived. Actually, Shakespeare wasn't written by Shakespeare but by another man named Shakespeare.
4. Macbeth and Lady Macbeth then suffer from quilt. In fact, they have so much quilt, they can't sleep at night. During the banquet scene, Lady Macbeth is afraid her husband will expose himself in front of his guests. Then Lady Macbeth gets kilt. The proof that the witches in *Macbeth* were supernatural is that no one could eat what they cooked.
5. Writing at the same time as Shakespeare was Miguel Cervantes. He wrote *Donkey Hote*. The next great author was John Milton. Milton wrote *Paradise Lost*. Then his wife died and he wrote *Paradise Regained*.
6. Edgar Allan Poe was a very curdling writer. He had an addition to alcohol. Because he was a very sad man, he wrote very sad stories. The reason he was so sad is that he was impudent.

7. When Arthur Dimmesdale felt guilt about his sin in *The Scarlet Letter*, he felt better when he went on the scaffold and relieved himself.
8. Emily Dickinson was a wreck loose from society.
9. In 1957, Eugene O'Neill won a Pullet Surprise.
10. *Lord of the Flies* is a story about a bunch of boys on an uninhibited desert island.

Top 10 Spelling Bloopers

1. On Thanksgiving Day we could smell the foul cooking.
2. In Pittsburgh they manufacture iron and steal.
3. If a tree falls in the dessert, does it make a sound?
4. Vestal virgins were pure and chased.
5. In midevil times most people were alliterate.
6. Joan of Arc was burnt to a steak.
7. They gave William IV a large funeral. It took six men to carry the beer.
8. I want to be a foreign exchange student because I would enjoy studding all over Europe.
9. Carbon dating allows us to determine the age of mommies in Egypt.
10. Yesterday, my father received a package by special devilry.

Top 10 College Admissions Bloopers

1. I am in the mist of choosing colleges.
2. If there is a single word to describe me, that word would be "profectionist."
3. I was abducted into the national honor society.
4. In my senior year I am serving as writing editor of the yearbook.
5. I can read, speak, and write Greek fluently. My other two sports are tennis and volleyball.
6. I would like to become a veterinarian. I have had some experience with animals. I have volunteered at dog kennels and cat houses.
7. Mathematics has hung like a stork around my neck.
8. I have made the horror role every semester.
9. I have taken many curses in literature and writing.
10. I like your college because it is private and very small in stature. I was discouraged to find out that I had been weight-listed and differed from your college.

Sunday School Bloopers

The Bible is full of many interesting charicatures.
–from a STUDENT ESSAY

Naming Names
A Sunday school teacher was talking about Christmas and the coming of Christ and she asked, "And what was Jesus's mother's name?"

"Mary," all said.

"Now what was his father's name?"

One little fellow raised his hand, "Virg."

"Virg? Where did you get that idea?"

"Well," answered the boy, "they always talk about the Virg 'n Mary."

Baby Steps
A Sunday school teacher asked her class why Joseph and Mary took Jesus with them to Jerusalem.

A small child replied, "They couldn't get a baby-sitter."

A Lot of Information
Another religion teacher was telling her class the story of Lot. "Lot was warned to take his wife and flee out of the city, but his wife looked back and she was turned to salt." She looked around the class, and one little girl tentatively raised her hand. "Yes?" said the teacher.

"I was wondering," said the girl, "what happened to the flea?"

A Pillar of Society

The Sunday school teacher was describing how Lot's wife looked back and turned into a pillar of salt, when little Jimmy interrupted. "My Mommy looked back once while she was driving," he announced triumphantly, "and she turned into a telephone pole!"

Wall Art

Another Bible teacher asked a student who knocked down the walls of Jericho. "It wasn't me!" insisted Vincent.

Give Him a Hand

Little Johnny was spending the weekend with his grandmother after a particularly trying week in kindergarten. His grandmother decided to take him to the park on Saturday morning. It had been snowing all night and everything was beautiful. His grandmother remarked, "Doesn't it look like an artist painted this scenery? Did you know God painted this just for you?"

Johnny said, "Yes, God did it and he did it left handed."

This confused his grandmother a bit, and she asked him, "What makes you say God did this with his left hand?"

"Well," said Johnny, "we learned at Sunday school last week that Jesus sits on God's right hand!"

The Old One-Two

When a Hebrew school teacher intoned, "The Lord our God is one," little Benjamin asked, "When will He be two?"

The Plane Truth

An art teacher in a Maine elementary school also taught Sunday school, where she had the little ones draw pictures of the Bible stories. Little Emma proudly presented her picture of the journey to Bethlehem. The drawing showed an airplane flying over the desert. In the passenger area were seated Joseph and Mary and baby Jesus.

"The drawing is fine," said the teacher, "but who's that up front flying the plane?"

Answered Emma, "Why that's Pontius the Pilot."

Another Vehicle

A religion teacher told her first-graders to draw a big picture of the story of Adam and Eve and the garden of Eden. One little boy drew a big car with God at the wheel driving Adam and Eve out of Paradise.

Grin and Bear It

When yet another teacher asked her student why there was a dog in the nativity drawing, the fledgling artist explained that it was a German shepherd. That dog has been joined in the gallery of Sunday school portraiture by a grinning bear with wandering eyes—Gladly, the Cross-Eyed Bear, of course.

Commandment Performance

A Sunday school teacher was discussing the Ten Commandments with her six-year-olds. After explaining the commandment to "Honor thy father and thy mother," she asked, "Is there a commandment that teaches us how to treat our brothers and sisters?"

Without missing a beat, one little boy answered, "Thou shall not kill."

It's in the Cards

A Sunday school teacher said to her children, "We have been learning how powerful kings and queens were in Bible times. But there is a higher power. Can anybody tell me what it is?"

One child blurted out, "Aces!"

On Command

When a Sunday school teacher asked his class to list the Ten Commandments in any order, one student offered, "3, 6, 1, 8, 4, 5, 9, 2, 10, and 7."

Excuses, Excuses

Excuuuuuse me!!!–STEVE MARTIN

The high school had a policy that the parents must call the school if a student was to be absent for the day. Madison decided to skip school and go to the mall with her friends. She waited until her parents had left for work and called the school herself.

"Hello, I'm calling to report that Madison Tyler is unable to come to school today because she is ill," Madison phoned in.

The school secretary asked, "I'm sorry to hear that. I'll note her absence. Who is this calling?"

"This is my mother."

In reality, most schools require excuse notes from parents. The following drastic measures were inadvertently taken in notes written by parents to excuse their children's absences from school:

"My son is under the doctor's care and should not take P.E. today," wrote a parent. "Please execute him."

"Please excuse Mary for being absent," wrote another parent. "She was sick and I had her shot."

Slaughtering the English language is a practice that is not limited only to students. An astonishing number of grownups blithely go about murdering the King's English without any inkling that they are committing a serious crime. Here are some actual excuse notes miscreated by actual moms and dads and received by actual teachers:

- Dear School: Please excuse John being absent on Jan. 28, 29, 30, 31, 32, and also 33.
- Please excuse Roland from P.E. for a few days. Yesterday he fell out of a tree and misplaced his hip.
- John has been absent because he had two teeth taken off his face.

- Carlos was absent yesterday because he was playing football. He was hurt in the growing part.
- Mary could not come to school because she has been bothered by very close veins.
- Stanley had to miss some school. He had an attack of whooping cranes in his chest.
- Please excuse Arlita from being absent on Friday because she broke her figure.
- Please accuse Michael for being absent yesterday.
- Please excuse Jimmy for being. It was his father's fault.
- I kept Billie home because she had to go Christmas shopping because I don't know what size she wear.
- Please excuse Harriet for missing school yesterday. We forgot to get the Sunday paper off the porch, and when we found it Monday, we thought it was Sunday.
- Please excuse my son's tardiness. I forgot to wake him up and I did not find him until I started making the beds.
- Please forgive Clarence for being absent from school the past few days. He was home sick from an operation. He had trouble and had to be serpent sized.
- Maryann was absent December 11–16 because she had a fever, sore throat, headache, and upset stomach. Her sister was also sick, fever and sore throat. Her brother had a low-grade fever and ached all over. I wasn't the best either, sore throat and fever. There must be the flu going around school. Her father even got hot last night.

Famous Excuse Notes
Now have a look at some excuse notes written by the parents of students who became famous or infamous. While the previous notes are real, these pun-in-cheek examples are made up:

Imaginary Students
- Please excuse Rip Van Winkle for missing the past twenty years of school. He overslept.
- Please excuse Goliath for his absence from school yesterday. He got stoned and developed a terrific headache.

- Please excuse King Kong for missing the past few days of class. He had to catch a plane.
- Please excuse Batboy from school for the rest of the week. He has to save Gotham City.
- Please excuse Spider-Boy for not handing in his homework. He got caught up exploring the Internet and surfing the web.
- Please excuse Dracula for missing the entire school year. We can't seem to stop him from staying up all night, and it's impossible to wake him up in the morning.
- Please excuse The Invisible Boy for his absence yesterday. We couldn't find him to send him off to school.
- Please excuse The Wolfboy from school for the next week. He is suffering from Irritable Howl Syndrome.

Real Students

- Please excuse George Washington from school. He had to go to the dentist to get his wooden teeth re-lacquered, and then he had to load up and bring in the cherry tree limbs from our backyard so we could use them as firewood.
- Kindly excuse Abraham Lincoln for the rest of the year. He has moved to a Gettysburg address.
- We request that you excuse Ralph Nader from school for the rest of the year. He has determined that the school bus is unsafe at any speed.
- Please excuse Peter Roget for missing school yesterday. He was sick, ill, unwell, stricken, run down, feeling queasy, yucky, punky, under the weather, down in the mouth, and green around the gills.
- Please excuse Isaac Newton from school for a few days while he recovers from a mild concussion. An apple fell on his head.
- We apologize that Salvador Dali was late to school. His watch melted, and he couldn't read the time.
- We must explain why Rin Tin Tin failed to hand in his book report. He ate his own homework.

9

A Teacher's Dictionary

The teacher is one who makes two ideas grow where only one grew before.
–ELBERT HUBBARD

Education's purpose is to replace an empty mind with an open one.
–MALCOLM FORBES

One could define *education* as:

- a torch that one generation kindles to light the way for the next;
- the transmission of civilization, the passing of the torch from one generation to the next;
- the discovery of something you didn't know you didn't know;
- the discovery of something you didn't know you knew;
- drilling abstract ideas into concrete heads;
- what you have left over when you subtract what you've forgotten from what you learned;
- a technique employed to open minds so that they may go from cocksure ignorance to thoughtful uncertainty;
- a progressive discovery of our own ignorance;
- bridging the gap between your ears;
- an effort to convert an empty mind into an open one.

Here's a start on a dictionary for teachers:

absent-minded. Why teachers take attendance.

adolescent. 1. hormones poured into sneakers. 2. A student who will spend twelve minutes studying for her history exam and twelve hours for her driver's license. 3. One who is well informed about anything he doesn't have to study. 4. One who has stopped asking questions because she knows all the answers.

absolute zero. The lowest grade that can be given on a test.

aftermath. The period following Algebra.

attention. What you should pay a teacher even if you have no money.

brain. A wonderful organ that starts working as soon as a student wakes up and stops working as soon as she is asked a question in class.

caffeine. A substance teachers wish would be available in intravenous form.

classroom. A place where the climate for learning promotes occasional brainstorms and bolts of enlightening.

college years. The only vacation a boy gets between his mother and his wife.

commencement. Both an ending and a beginning.

contest. An examination taken by a prisoner.

detention. What causes de stress: "De love of teaching outweighs detention that comes with de job."

diploma. De person who fixes de pipes.

drama teacher. A stage coach who produces class acts.

English teacher. An inmate in the House of Correction.

faculty meeting. A debate in which teachers take hours to take minutes.

first grade teacher. One who knows how to make little things count.

Geometry. What an acorn says when it's grown up.

head of the school orchestra. A super conductor.

hindsight. A talent that helps a teacher to avoid sitting on tacks placed on her chair by mischievous students.

hooky. When a boy lets his mind wander—and then follows it.

homework. 1. schoolwork to go. 2. skull-drudgery. 3. schoolwork often completed on a bus.

hunger. A condition generated by five minutes of continuous studying.

lecture. An occasion when students numb one end to benefit the other.

lecturer. 1. Someone with his finger in the air, his tongue in your ear, and his faith in your patience. 2. Someone who talks in other people's sleep.

physics. What constipated scientists take.

pop quiz. Paternity test.

school. 1. Something to do between weekends. 2. A building with four walls and tomorrow inside.

slide rules. Instructions for the school playground.

spring break. When students work on their tans and teachers work on their sanity.

Statistics teacher. The Wizard of Odds.

student athlete. An oxymoron.

summer school. A viable alternative to a summer job.

teacher. 1. Someone who affects eternity 2. A compulsive sharer. 3. Someone who strives to make himself progressively unnecessary. 4. A child's third parent. 5. Someone who swore she would starve before teaching, and who has been doing both ever since. 6. A life changer.

teachers. United Mind Workers.

team teaching. Instructing a band of athletes.

tutor. A horn player in a marching band.

understudy. To prepare inadequately for an examination.

unprincipled. A headless school.

vacation. A time when parents realize that teachers aren't paid enough.

The Creation of Teachers

There is a loftier ambition than merely to stand high in the world.
It is to stoop down and lift mankind a little higher.
–HENRY VAN DYKE

I am only one, but still I am one.
I cannot do everything, but still I can do something;
and because I cannot do everything,
I will not refuse to do the something that I can do.
–EDWARD EVERETT HALE

Real teachers are medical marvels.* Real teachers are written up in medical journals for the size and elasticity of their bladders and kidneys. They have eyes in the backs of their heads and the preternatural ability to hear someone in the class whispering. Real teachers have stiff necks from writing on the blackboard while keeping their eyes on their students. They are immune to the smells of collective bad breath and throw-up, kids' viruses, and the sound of chalk squeaking across a blackboard.

Real teachers are able to memorize thirty-six names (including nicknames) within the first week of school. Real teachers often remember your name at a twenty-fifth class reunion (and you remember theirs!). Real teachers know every knock-knock joke ever created. They actually know the differences between glue and mucilage and oak tag and poster board.

---

*In reality, teaching can be hazardous to your health. For example, teachers must talk for many hours each day, often in loud settings and often at high volume. As a result of such vocal stress, as many as 47 percent of American teachers experience voice problems on any given day (I'm one of them), and 10 percent of teachers have been forced out of the profession because of damage to their vocal cords.

Real teachers learn to inhale their lunch in as little as three minutes. They actually like fruit cup. Real teachers are able to consume anything left over in the teachers' room. Real teachers laugh uncontrollably when people refer to that room as a "lounge." Real teachers buy Excedrin and Advil at Sam's Club.

Real teachers have a highly developed sixth sense. Real teachers know exactly how many Oreo cookies are in a package and how many jelly beans are in a jar. Real teachers can predict exactly which parents will show up at open house. Real teachers know when it's a full moon without having to look outside. Real teachers know that the first class disruption they see is probably the second one that has occurred. Real teachers can "sense" gum. Real teachers never sit down without first checking the seat of the chair. Real teachers hear the heartbeats of crisis.

How were such amazing human beings created?

On the sixth day, God created men and women.

On the seventh day, He rested.

Not so much to recuperate, but rather to prepare Himself for the work He was going to do on the next day. For it was on that day—the eighth day—that God created The First Teacher.

This First Teacher, though modeled on ordinary men and women, was special. God made The Teacher more durable than other men and women—fit to arise at the crack of dawn and to go to bed deep into darkness, with no rest in between.

God made The Teacher tough, to be able to work in an airtight classroom for six hours on a rainy day with twenty-five or more balls of energy bouncing off walls—tough to run all day on the fuel of coffee and cookies. And The Teacher had to be tough to correct more than a hundred term papers over Easter vacation.

And into The Teacher God poured a generous portion of patience. Patience when a student asks to repeat the directions The Teacher has just repeated for someone else. The Teacher is endowed with great understanding when the children forget their lunch money for the fourth day in a row, when one-third of the class fails a test, and when the textbooks haven't arrived yet.

And God gave The Teacher a spacious heart. A heart big enough to love the child who screams, "I hate this class! It's boring!" A heart big enough to love the child who runs out of the classroom at the end of the period without so much as a "goodbye," let alone a "thank you." A heart big enough to embrace lonely students—the six-year-old boy who has no friends in the classroom, the sixteen-year-old girl who has not been asked to the prom. A heart big enough to devote more time for others than for itself.

And God gave The Teacher an accordion spine that could elongate and contract itself so that The Teacher could stand above all students, yet be at their level. And God endowed The Teacher with six pairs of hands, to accomplish a dozen tasks at once.

And with those six pairs of hands came four pairs of eyes. One pair to see students for what they are and not what others have labeled them. Another pair of eyes in the back of The Teacher's head to see what should not be seen, but what must be known. A third pair in front to look at the child as he or she "acts out" in order to reflect, "I understand and I still believe in you," without so much as saying a word to the child. And a fourth pair of eyes inside The Teacher's mind to see the future and to prepare the students to reap the full fruits of that future.

And on The Teacher's cheek God placed a gleaming tear. The Teacher's glowing tear was for the joy and pride of seeing a child accomplish even the smallest task. The shining tear came from the pain of not being able to reach some children and the disappointment those children feel in themselves. And the glistening tear became tears when, at the end of a school year, the time came to say goodbye to those students and to get ready to welcome a new class.

A Teacher's Prayer

Lord, let me be just what my students need.
If they need someone to trust, let me be trustworthy.
If they need sympathy, let me sympathize.
If they need love (and they do need love), let me love in
    full measure.
Let me not be enkindled to anger easily, Lord, but let me be just.
Let my justice be tempered with Your mercy.
Let them see me as strong and good and honest and loving.
And let me be as strong and good and honest and loving as I look to them.
Help me to counsel the anxious, assure the afraid,
Reach beneath the covering of the shy,
Soothe the rambunctious with gentleness,
And help the undiscovered to discover themselves.

Permit me to inspire those placed in my charge
So that learning will not stop at the classroom door,
So that learning will be their lifelong adventure.
And, Dear Lord, help me to learn the lessons they teach.

A Teacher's Tale

Teaching is the greatest act of optimism.–COLLEEN WILCOX

The art of teaching is the art of assisting discovery.
–MARK VAN DOREN

*We never forget our best teachers—those who imbued us
with a deeper understanding or an enduring passion,
the ones we come back to visit years after graduating,
the educators who opened doors and altered the course of our lives.*
—CLAUDIA WALLACE

Her name was Mrs. Thompson. As she stood in front of her fifth grade class on the very first day of school, she told the children a lie. Like most teachers, she looked at her students and said that she loved them all the same. But that was impossible, because there in the front row, slumped in his seat, was a little boy named Teddy Stoddard.

Mrs. Thompson immediately saw that the boy didn't play well with the other children. His clothes were messy and he needed a bath. And Teddy could be unpleasant. It got to the point where Mrs. Thompson would actually take delight in marking his papers with a broad red pen, making bold X's and then putting a big *F* at the top of his papers.

At the school where Mrs. Thompson taught, she was required to review each child's past records and she put Teddy's off until last. However, when she explored his file, she was in for a surprise.

Teddy's first-grade teacher wrote, "Teddy is a bright child with a ready laugh. He does his work neatly and has good manners. He is a joy to be around."

His second grade teacher wrote, "Teddy is an excellent student, well liked by his classmates, but he is troubled because his mother has a terminal illness and life at home is a struggle."

His third grade teacher wrote, "His mother's death had been hard on him. He tries to do his best, but his father doesn't show much interest, and his home life will soon affect him if some steps aren't taken."

Teddy's fourth grade teacher wrote, "Teddy is withdrawn and doesn't show much interest in school. He doesn't have many friends and he sometimes sleeps in class."

By now, Mrs. Thompson realized the problem, and she was ashamed of herself. She felt even worse when her students brought her Christmas presents wrapped in beautiful ribbons and bright paper, except for Teddy's. His present was clumsily wrapped in the heavy, brown paper that he got from a grocery bag. Mrs. Thompson took pains to open it with the other presents.

Some of the children started to laugh when she found a rhinestone bracelet with some of the stones missing, and a bottle that was one quarter-full of perfume. But she stifled the children's laughter when she exclaimed how pretty the bracelet was, putting it on, and dabbing some of the perfume on her wrist.

Teddy Stoddard stayed after school that day just long enough to say, "Mrs. Thompson, today you smelled just like my mother used to."

After the children left, she cried for an hour. On that very day, she quit teaching reading, writing, and arithmetic. Instead, she began to teach children.

Mrs. Thompson paid particular attention to Teddy. As she worked with him, his mind seemed to come alive. The more she encouraged him, the faster he responded. By the end of the year, Teddy had become one of the best pupils in the class. Despite her lie that she would love all the children the same, Teddy became one of her favorites.

A year later, she found a note under her door, from Teddy, telling her that she was still the best teacher he ever had in his whole life. Six years went by before she got another note from Teddy. He then wrote that he had finished high school, third in his class, and she was still the best teacher he ever had in his whole life.

Four years after that, she got another letter, saying that while things had been tough at times, he'd stayed in school, had stuck with it, and would soon graduate from college with the highest of honors. He assured Mrs. Thompson that she was still the best and favorite teacher he ever had in his whole life.

Four more years passed and yet another letter came. This time Teddy explained that after he got his bachelor's degree, he decided to go a little further. The letter explained that she was still the best and favorite teacher he ever had. But now his name was a little longer the letter was signed "Theodore F. Stoddard, MD."

The story doesn't end there. You see, there was yet another letter that spring. Teddy said he'd met this girl and was going to be married. He explained that his father had died a couple of years ago and he was wondering if Mrs. Thompson might agree to sit in the place at the wedding that was usually reserved for the mother of the groom.

Of course, Mrs. Thompson did. And guess what? She wore that bracelet, the one with several rhinestones missing. And she made sure she was wearing the perfume that Teddy remembered his mother wearing on their last Christmas together. They hugged each other, and Dr. Stoddard whispered in Mrs. Thompson's ear, "Thank you, Mrs. Thompson, for believing in me. Thank you so much for making me feel important and showing me that I could make a difference."

Mrs. Thompson, with tears welling from her eyes, whispered back, "Teddy, you have it all wrong. You were the one who taught me that I could make a difference. I didn't know how to teach until I met you."

Educated Bumper Snickers

True terror is to wake up one morning and discover
that your high school class is running the country.
–KURT VONNEGUT, JR.

- Teachers Have a Lot of Class.
- I Teach. What's Your Superpower?
- Teachers Change the World One Child at a Time.
- Teachers Make a World of Difference.
- Teachers Are Works of Heart.
- Teaching Is Heart Work.
- School
  's Cool.
- My Teacher Deserves More Than Just an Apple.
  She Deserves the Whole Tree.
- The Dog Ate My Lesson Plans.
- Don't Make Me Use My Teacher Voice!
- Pre-School Teachers Love the Little Things in Life.
- You Can't Scare Me. I'm a Teacher.
- My Teacher Talks to Herself in Class.
  She Thinks We're Listening.
- Discover Wildlife. Become a Teacher.
- Teaching Means Commitment.
  So Does Insanity.

- Insanity is Inherited.
  You Get It from Your Students.
- Education Is National Security.
- Experience is a Hard Teacher.
  She Gives the Tests First
  And the Lessons Afterwards.
- Old Teachers Never Die. They Just Grade Away
  And Lose Their Principals, Their Faculties, and Their Class.
- Old Teachers Never Die. They Just Get
  Detested, Degraded, and Declassified.
- Teachers Don't Accept "Can't."
  Teachers are "Can" Openers.
- Behind Every Successful Student
  Stands an Exhausted Teacher.
- Students Learn their ABCs at LMN-tary School.
- Home Sweet Homeroom.
- I'd Rather Be Teaching.
- Warning: Driver May Be Grading Papers.
- To Learn Well Is a Blessing.
  To Teach Well Is a Gift.
- If You Can Read This, Thank a Teacher.
- I Went to School to Become a Wit,
  But I Only Got Halfway Through.
- Practice What You Teach.
- Have You Hugged a Teacher Today?
- Endangered Species:
  Male Elementary School Teacher.
- History Teachers Love Dead People.
- Geology Professors Rock!
- Teachers Are Angels in Training.
- A Teacher Takes a Hand,
  Touches a Mind, and Opens a Heart.
- What a Teacher Writes on the Blackboard
  Of Life Can Never Be Erased.

Lists Every Teacher Should Know

The highest result of education is tolerance.
–HELEN KELLER

The most beautiful thing in the world
is the conjunction of learning and inspiration.
–WANDA LANDOWSKI

10 Educational Words

1. **curriculum.** From the Latin *currere*, "to run." The metaphor here is of carriages driven around a race course.
2. **education.** From the Latin *educare*, "to bring up."
3. **principal.** From the Latin *principalis,* "first in importance." Before principals became solely administrators, they were called "principal teachers."
4. **teacher.** Rooted in the Old English word *tacn*, related to *token* and meaning "symbol" and "to show."
5. **pupil.** From the Latin *pupillus*, "small boy."
6. **sophomore.** Second-year students get their name from *sophism*, the Greek word for "becoming wise," and the English word *more*, "fool." Thus, a sophomore is an oxymoron, meaning "wise fool." How true.
7. **kindergarten.** From the German for "child's garden." Originally *kleinkenderbeschaftigungsanstalt*, which means "institution where small children are occupied," but even the Germans found that to be a mouthful.
8. **liberal arts.** Not from the idea of political progressivism, but from the concept of the liberation (Latin *liber*, "free") those disciplines

are meant to confer upon the intellect. The seven liberal arts were divided into two groups, the Trivium (grammar, rhetoric, and logic) and the Quadrivium (arithmetic, geometry, music, and astronomy). *Trivium* and *Quadrivium* in Latin mean "the three ways/roads" and "the four ways/roads" respectively. As the Trivium was studied first, it was considered more elementary than the Quadrivium. This attitude gave rise to the words *trivia* and *trivial*.

9. **school.** From the Greek *skhole*, meaning "leisure." In the original schools, only the children of the idle rich had time to devote to study. The curriculum considered appropriate for working men's children was labeled the servile or mechanical arts.

10. **university.** From the Latin word *universitas*, "aggregate, whole, the universe."

50 Famous People Who Were Once Teachers

The lyrics to the soaring song "America the Beautiful" were written by Katherine Lee Bates (1859–1929), a professor of English at Wellesley College. On a trip to the Rocky Mountains in Colorado in 1893, she was inspired by the view from Pike's Peak to create what many people feel should be our national anthem.

West Virginia schoolteacher Anna Jarvis (1864–1948) campaigned tirelessly for and succeeded in establishing Mother's Day as a national holiday. She never married and had no children.

You never can tell who was once a teacher or what else your teacher may one day become. These luminaries were all teachers before they achieved wider celebrity:

• historical figures Thomas Paine, Nathan Hale, Harriet Beecher Stowe, Clara Barton, Carry Nation, Benito Mussolini, Golda Meir, and Henry Kissinger;

• American presidents John Adams, Andrew Jackson, James Garfield, Woodrow Wilson, and Lyndon Johnson;

• First Ladies Caroline Harrison, Abigail Fillmore, Grace Coolidge, and Pat Nixon;

• composers and lyricists Franz Liszt, W. C. Handy, and Nikolai Rimsky-Korsakov, as well as Mildred and Patty Hill, who created "Happy Birthday to You," the most sung song in history;

• singers Roberta Flack, Art Garfunkel, Kris Kristofferson, Sting, and Sheryl Crow;

• entertainers Margaret Hamilton, who played the Wicked Witch of the West in *The Wizard of Oz*; Sam Levenson; Andy Griffith; Sylvester Stallone; and Billy Crystal;

- inventors and scientists Louis Braille, ~~Marie Curie, and Albert~~ Einstein;
- writers Samuel Johnson, Walt Whitman, Louisa May Alcott, Aldous Huxley, James Joyce, D. H. Lawrence, Robert Frost, George Orwell, J. R. R. Tolkien, C. S. Lewis, William Golding, Stephen King, Frank McCourt, and J. K. Rowling.

Top 10 Reasons to Become a Teacher

1. You get to practice the great art of pedagogy.
2. You get to teach children such life skills as tying their shoes, zipping their jackets, and snapping their fingers.
3. You get to teach Roman numerals; "*I* before *e*, except after *c* or when sounded like *a*, as in *neighbor* and *weigh*"; The Dewey Decimal System; and the crucial differences between participles and gerunds.
4. You get the chance to return to the place where you were long ago humiliated, this time with power.
4. You know all the answers on the test.
6. You get the chance to discipline tomorrow's leaders. Even the president of the United States got yelled at once by a teacher.
7. Tom Hanks mentioned his teacher in his Academy Award acceptance speech. It could happen to you!
8. You can learn all the tricks of how to get your own kids into Harvard.
9. Guaranteed parking space every single workday.
10. Free apples.

10 Things You'll Never Hear a Teacher Say

1. "Thank goodness for these evaluations. They keep me focused."
2. "Thank goodness for those twenty-minute lunch periods."
3. "I just love the food they serve in the school cafeteria."
4. "I bet all the people in our administration really miss teaching."
5. "Why don't we have more faculty meetings?"
6. "Isn't it great that the parents of my most troubled students come so regularly to parent-teacher conferences?"
7. "Gosh, the bathroom smells so fresh and clean."
8. "I think the discipline around here is just a little too strict."
9. "It's Friday already?"
10. "I can't believe they pay me so much to do this!"

Figures of Teach

The dream begins with a teacher who believes in you,
who tugs and pushes and leads you to the next plateau,
sometimes poking you with a sharp stick called truth.
–WILLIAM ARTHUR WARD

Life is a school, and we are here to learn. The challenges and problems we encounter are simply part of the curriculum. They appear and they fade away, but the lessons we learn last a lifetime.

The foregoing paragraph is a metaphor, a word that in Greek originally meant "carry beyond." A metaphor is a figure of speech that compares two objects or ideas that are different from each other but turn out to be alike in a significant way. Here are my favorite "figures of teach" that illuminate the role of education in our lives:

- Genius without education is like silver in the mine.–*Benjamin Franklin*
- No bubble is so iridescent or floats longer than one blown by a beloved teacher.–*Sir William Osler*
- Don't judge each day by the harvest you reap, but by the seeds that you plant.–*Robert Louis Stevenson*
- Education is light; lack of it is darkness.–*Russian proverb*
- We cannot hold a torch to light another's path without brightening our own.–*Ben Sweetland*
- A teacher is the candle that lights the way for others in consuming itself.–*Giovanni Ruffini*
- Teachers can't burn out if they aren't on fire.–*Anita Voelker*

- Every time you stop a school, you will have to build a jail. What you gain at one end you lose at the other. It's like feeding a dog on its own tail. It won't fatten the dog.–*Mark Twain*
- He who opens a school door, closes a prison.–*Victor Hugo*
- He who has imagination with no education has wings but no feet.–*French proverb*
- Give a man a fish, and he will eat for a day. Teach a man to fish, and he will eat for the rest of his life.–*Chinese proverb*
- If you plan for a year, plant a seed. If you plan for ten years, plant a tree. If you plan for a hundred years, teach the people.–*Kuan Chung*
- None of us got where we are solely by pulling ourselves up by our bootstraps. We got here because somebody bent down and helped us pick up our boots.–*Thurgood Marshall*
- Minds are like parachutes. They function only when open.–*James Dewar*
- Ideas are like umbrellas. If they are left lying about, they are peculiarly liable to a change of ownership.–*Tom Kettle*
- The whole purpose of education is to turn mirrors into windows.–*Sydney J. Harris*
- The primary purpose of a liberal education is to make one's mind a pleasant place in which to spend one's time.–*Sydney J. Harris*
- Education is not filling a bucket, but lighting a fire.–*William Butler Yeats*
- In teaching it is the method and not the content that is the message—the drawing out, not the pumping in.–*Ashley Montagu*
- The teacher who is indeed wise does not bid you to enter the house of his wisdom but rather leads you to the threshold of your mind.–*Kahlil Gibran*
- A mind that is stretched by a new experience never goes back to its old dimensions.–*Oliver Wendell Holmes*
- Spoonfeeding teaches us nothing but the shape of the spoon. –*E. M. Forster*
- A teacher who is attempting to teach without inspiring the pupil with a desire to learn is hammering on cold iron.–*Horace Mann*

- All kids are gifted, some just open their packages earlier than others.–*Michael Carr*

- A truly great teacher is perpetually rocking the boat in the cause of furthering the waves of understanding that flood over the walls of defense and denial built up around young people's thirsty minds.–*Daniel Mark Childs*

- Native ability without education is like a tree without fruit. –*Aristippus*

- 'Tis education forms the common mind;
  Just as the twig is bent the tree's inclined.

  –Alexander Pope

- "Teaching to the test" is a practice likened to memorizing an eye chart. With enough drill and rote work, even a person with 20/150 vision can rattle off E-F-P-T-O-Z. Of course, that doesn't mean that the person can see.–*Meredith Scrivener*

- A teacher is a compass that activates the magnets of curiosity, knowledge, and wisdom in the pupils.–*Terri Guillemets*

- Education is the horse. Experience is the jockey.–*Clark Gable*

Metaphors Be With You!

Students Say the Darnedest Things

I got an A in philosophy because I proved that my professor didn't exist.
–JUDY TENUTA

I (your teacherly author) once spent a terrific day working with fourth and fifth graders at Adobe Bluffs Elementary School in Poway, California, as a visiting lecturer about the many joys of language. Kids that age respond enthusiastically to puns, palindromes, and other kinds of language fun. In fact, the children made posters to celebrate my coming, including the statements "Richard Lederer, the Famous Writer" and "Richard Lederer, the Popular Speaker."

But my favorite placard read: "Richard Lederer, the Wanted Comedian."

It boggles the mind, tickles the funny bone, and flabbers the gast what comes out of the mouths of Babes in School-land:

Teacher Beware
The little boy was getting poor marks in school. One day he tapped his teacher on the shoulder and said, "I don't want to scare you, but my daddy says if I don't get better grades, somebody is going to get a spanking."

The Good Husband
A third grade teacher was getting to know her pupils on the first day of school. She turned to one little girl and asked, "What does your daddy do?"

The girl replied, "Whatever my mommy tells him to do."

Progress Report

Teacher: Winnie, name one important thing that we didn't have ten years ago but have now.

Winnie: Me!

Left Back

Said a second-grade pupil, "I really liked your class, Miss Jansen. I'm sorry you're not smart enough to teach us next year."

Generation Gap

Working as a computer instructor for an adult-education program at a community college, the teacher was keenly aware of the gap in computer knowledge between generations.

His observations were confirmed the day a new student walked into our library area and glanced at the encyclopedia volumes stacked on a bookshelf. "What are all these books?" he asked.

Somewhat surprised, the teacher explained that they were encyclopedias. "Really?" the student said. "Someone printed out the whole thing?"

Disaster

A third grader came into the classroom in tears. The teacher asked her what was wrong. The little girl answered, "I wrote down the wrong homework assignment, and wasted the whole evening studying something I don't need to know until next week!"

A Colorful Explanation

The kindergarten teacher asked her students what color they would get if they mixed blue and yellow. A little boy immediately shouted, "Green!" The teacher, impressed with the quick response, asked the boy how he knew.

"My mommy puts this blue stuff in the potty, and when I do a pee pee, it turns green."

Making Change

The new librarian decided that instead of checking out children's books by writing the names of borrowers on the book cards herself, she would have the youngsters sign their own names. She would then tell them they were signing a contract for returning the books on time.

Her first customer was a second-grader, who looked surprised to see a new librarian. He brought four books to the desk and shoved them across to her giving her his name as he did so. The librarian pushed the books back and told him to sign them out.

The boy laboriously printed his name on each book card and then handed them to her and said, "You're different."

When the librarian asked how she was different, the boy said, "That other librarian we had could write."

Field Trip

Ray's preschool class went on a field trip to the fire station. The firefighter giving the presentation held up a smoke detector and asked the class: "Does anyone know what this is?"

Ray's hand shot up, and the firefighter called on him. "That's how Mommy knows supper is ready!"

Show and Tell

An elementary school teacher from Miami remembers this Oscar-worthy birth tableau from one of her pupils:

Usually, show-and-tell is pretty tame. Children bring in pet, turtles, model airplanes, pictures of fish they catch, stuff like that. And I never ever place any boundaries or limitations on them. If they want to lug it to school and talk about it, they're welcome.

Well, one day this little girl, Anna, a very bright, very outgoing child, takes her turn and waddles up to the front of the class with a pillow stuffed under her sweater. She holds up a snapshot of an infant and says, "This is Luke, my baby brother, and I'm going to tell you about his birth day. First, Mom and Dad made him as a symbol of their love, and then Dad put a seed in my mom's stomach, and Luke grew in there. He ate for nine months through an umbrella cord."

Anna is standing there with her hands on the pillow, and I'm trying not to laugh and wishing I had my camcorder with me. The children are watching her in amazement.

"Then, about two Saturdays ago, my mom starts saying and going 'Oh, oh, oh!'" Anna puts a hand behind her back and groans. "She walked around the house for, like an hour, 'Oh, oh, oh!'" Now the child is doing this hysterical duck walk; holding her back and groaning.

"My dad called the middle wife. She delivers babies, but she doesn't have a sign on the car like the Domino's man. They got my mom to lie down in bed like this." Anna lies down with her back against the wall.

"And then, pop! My mom had this bag of water she kept in there in case he got thirsty, and it just blew up and spilled all over the bed, like *psshhheew!*" This child is sitting on the floor with her little hands miming water flowing away.

"Then the middle wife starts saying, 'Push, push, and breathe, breathe.' They started counting, but never even got past ten. All of a sudden, out comes my brother. He's covered in yucky stuff. They said it was from Mom's play center, so there must be a lot of stuff inside there for him to do."

Then Anna stood up, took a big theatrical bow and returned to her seat. I'm sure I applauded the loudest. Ever since then, if it's show-and-tell day, I bring my camcorder to class, just in case another Anna comes along.

Jumping to Confusions

WANTED: Private school has a position open for science teacher. Must be certified or certifiable.
—ACTUAL CLASSIFIED AD

The Son Shines Bright
A mother who drove a city bus attended an open house at her third-grader's school. When she met the teacher, he seemed amused and directed her to where her child's work was displayed.

An essay tacked up in a prominent position, titled "My Mom," read: "I like my mom because she is neat and pretty and tells everyone where to get off."

Head of School
A woman approached a new student at an elementary school and introduced herself saying, "Hello, I'm the principal here."

"No, you're not," replied the little girl. "You're the princessipal."

Biology Lesson
A teacher and her kindergarten students were studying mammals. One little boy asked, "Miss Cindy, are we considered mammals?"

"Why yes, Johnny, we are mammals."

One little girl added, "But aren't some of us femammals?"

Noteworthy
The third graders were attending their first music lesson, and the teacher was trying to begin at the beginning. She drew a musical staff on the blackboard and asked Jennifer to come up and write a note on it. The little girl went to the blackboard, looked thoughtful for a minute, wrote: "Dear Aunt Mary, just a short note to tell you I'm in the third grade now."

That's Life

During an especially trying time in the classroom, a teacher shrugged her shoulders and sighed, *"C'est la vie."*

Her pupils all shouted, *"La vie!"*

Raise Your Hand

On the first day of school, the kindergarten teacher said, "If anyone has to go to the bathroom, hold up two fingers."

A little voice in the back of the room asked, "How will that help?"

Boot-Eek!

A nursery school teacher had spent half an hour dressing her kiddies for their outdoor playtime, pulling on boots, zipping and unbuttoning coats, matching mittens and gloves. As she finished struggling with Jennifer's boots, she let out a sigh of relief. Then Jennifer tugged on her arm. "These boots aren't mine, teacher."

With a groan the teacher knelt down and pulled off the boots. "Do you know whose boots these are, Jennifer?"

"Sure. They're my sister's. Mom makes me wear them anyway."

Right on the Money

A fourth-grade teacher was giving her pupils a lesson in logic. "Here is the situation," she said. "A man is standing up in a boat in the middle of a river, fishing. He loses his balance, falls in, and begins splashing and yelling for help. His wife hears the commotion, knows he can't swim, and runs down to the bank. Why do you think she ran to the bank?"

A little girl raised her hand and asked, "To draw out all his savings?"

Unsung Hero

The sixth-grade music class had just started when one student asked the teacher, "Are we going to sing with musical accompaniment today, or Acapulco?"

Grammar Watching

A teacher came to the home of one of her pupils. When the little girl answered the door, the teacher asked, "Are your parents in?"

"They was in, but they is out now," replied the little girl.

"Where's your grammar?" asked the teacher, shocked.

"In the front room watching the TV."

The School Family

I speak to you not just as a president, but as a father when I say that responsibility for our children's education must begin at home.
–BARACK OBAMA

School is always in session.
–PHILIP ALLEN

I was homeschooled. The cat never stood a chance against me in dodgeball.
–ERIC ROTH

My kid drives me nuts.
For three years now, he goes to a private school.
He won't tell me where it is.
–RODNEY DANGERFIELD

Ms. Jones had been giving her second-grade students a lesson on science. She had explained about magnets and showed how they would pick up nails and other bits of iron. Now it was question time and she asked, "My name begins with the letter *m,* and I pick up things. What am I?"

A little boy on the front row said, "You're a mother."

Mothers and fathers play an exceedingly important role in the education of their children. Indeed, the primary responsibility for a child's education is "apparent."

Family Genealogy

"Mom, my teacher asked me today if I had any brothers or sisters who will be coming to school," explained young Henry.

"That's nice of her to take such an interest in you, dear. What did she say to you when you told her that you're an only child?"

"She just said, 'Thank goodness!'"

A Waste of Time

Cindy had just finished her first week of school when she announced to her mother, "I'm just wasting my time there. I can't read, I can't write, and they don't let me talk."

Day Trading

When Frank was in sixth grade, he took peanut-butter-and-jelly sandwiches to school every day. His mother finally asked him if he was sick of them. He replied, "Heck no. They're the best kind for trading."

Creative Writing

A little girl was pounding away at her father's computer. She told him she was writing a story for school.

"What's it about?"

"I don't know. I can't read."

Crime and Punishment

A little girl came home from school and said to her mother, "Mommy, today in school I was punished for something that I didn't do."

The mother exclaimed, "That's terrible! I'm going to have a talk with your teacher about this. By the way, what was it that you didn't do?"

"My homework."

Out of Focus

Justin had worn glasses since the age of three. When he was in the first grade, he came home one day very distressed. His mother asked, "Justin, what happened today to upset you so much?"

He answered, "It's not fair! I'm not allowed to go to the library."

His mother became very concerned and asked, "Why aren't you allowed to go to the library?"

Tearfully he replied, "Because, in order to go to the library you have to have supervision, and I wear glasses!"

In the Beginning I

Jane came home from her first day at school. Jane's mother asked her how her day had gone. "It was all right, except for some lady named teacher who kept spoiling all our fun."

In the Beginning II

Another kindergartener came home from his first school day, and his mother asked him, "What did you learn in school today?"

"Not enough," replied the little boy. "They say I have to go back tomorrow."

In the Beginning III
Dad was talking with his son about the boy's first day in kindergarten. "What did you learn today?"

"I learned to say 'yes sir' and 'no sir,'" the boy replied.

"You did?" asked the father.

"Uh huh."

American Sign Language
Daughter: Dad, can you write in the dark?

Father: I think so. What do you want me to write?

Daughter: Your name on this report card.

It Doesn't Add Up
Son: Mom, today I got a hundred in two subjects.

Mother: That's wonderful. In what two subjects?

Son: Well, I got a 50 in Math and a 50 in Science.

Back When
Father: When I was your age; I thought nothing of walking five miles to school.

Son: I agree, I don't think much of it myself either.

The Perils of Homework
Son: Dad, I'm tired of doing homework.

Father: Now son, hard work never killed anyone yet.

Son: I know, Dad, but I don't want to be the first.

Weather or Not
Daughter: Great news! The teacher said we'd have a test today rain or shine!

Mother: What's so great about that?

Daughter: It's snowing.

Sorely Missed
Mother: Why did you get such a low mark on that test?

Son: Because of absence.

Mother: You mean you were absent on the day of the test?

Son: No, but the kid who sits next to me was.

Give It a Try

Son: Dad, I'm late for baseball practice. Can you please do my homework for me?

Father: Son, it just wouldn't be right.

Son: That's okay. Could you at least try?

History Lesson

Student: My teacher thinks I'm going to be famous.

Mother: Why?

Student: She said if she heard another peep out of me, I'd be history.

Sex Education?

A second grader came home from school and said, "Mom, guess what? We learned how to make *babies* today."

Mother, more than a little surprised, tried to keep her cool. "That's interesting," she gulped. "How *do* you make babies?"

"It's simple," replied the girl. "You just change the *y* to *i* and add *es*."

Get Up and Go

Early one morning, a mother went in to get her son out of bed. "Wake up. It's time to go to school!"

"But why, Mom? I don't want to go."

"Give me two reasons why you don't want to go."

"Well, for one thing, the kids hate me, and the teachers hate me, too!"

"Oh, that's no reason not to go to school. Come on now and get ready."

"Mom! Give me two reasons why I should go to school."

"Well, for one thing, you're fifty-two years old. And for another, you're the principal!"

Appearances Can Be Deceiving

Teacher: Mrs. Benson, I asked you in to discuss your son Billy's appearance in the classroom.

Mrs. Benson: Why? What's wrong with Billy's appearance in the classroom?

Teacher: He hasn't made one since September.

The Classroom Lives of Real Teachers

If a doctor, lawyer, or dentist had forty people in his office at one time,
all of whom had different needs
and some of whom didn't want to be there and were causing trouble,
and the doctor, lawyer, or dentist, without assistance, had to treat them all
with professional excellence for nine months,
then he might have some conception of the classroom teacher's job.
–DONALD D. QUINN

A lesson plan is perfect until the children arrive–JANE WARDROP

Teachers are the most powerful people in the world
because who else can tell two hundred other people
exactly when they can go to the toilet?
–ALBERT SHANKER

Rushing to work, Branita drove too fast and was pulled over by a highway patrolman. The trooper noticed that her shirt was emblazoned with the name of a local high school. "I teach math there," Branita explained.

The trooper smiled, and said, "Okay, here's a problem. A teacher is speeding down the highway at sixteen miles per hour over the limit. At $12 for every mile, plus $40 court costs, plus the rise in her insurance, what's her total cost?"

Branita replied, "Taking that total, subtracting the low salary I receive, multiplying by the number of kids who fear math, then adding the fact that none of us would be anywhere without teachers, I'd say zero."

The officer handed the teacher back her license. "I once had a teacher who taught me to enjoy math," he confessed. "Please slow down."

Branita is a real teacher, and real teachers know their way around the classroom:

Real teachers grade papers during commercials, in faculty meetings, in the car, in the bathroom, at social and athletic events, and sometimes even in church and synagogue. Real teachers know the difference between what should be graded, and what should never see the light of day.

Real teachers know that secretaries and custodians really run the school. Real teachers have the assistant principals' and counselors' home phone numbers. Real teachers know that rules do not apply to them. Real teachers do not take "no" for an answer unless it is written in a complete sentence. Real teachers really care that you learn the capital of Idaho. Real teachers never conjugate the verbs *lie* and *lay* to ninth graders. Real teachers cheer when they discover that April 1 does not fall on a school day. Real teachers plan their seating charts so that the shorter pupils can't hide behind the taller ones. Real teachers have already heard every possible homework excuse. They know that dogs are carnivores and not "homework papervores."

Real teachers always have time to listen. Real teachers have their best conferences in parking lots. Real teachers understand the importance of making sure that every kid gets a valentine. Real teachers vow to do a better job than the teachers they had. Real teachers know they teach students, not subjects. When a real teacher meets a parent, she or he instantly knows the answer to "Why is my student like that?" Real teachers understand that they can't reach all their students, but that doesn't stop them from trying.

Real teachers get a lot more valentines than the rest of us. Real teachers are some of the most courageous, caring, and committed people you've ever met. Real teachers lovingly labor in the most unheralded, labor-intensive, multitasking, exhausting, income-challenged, and rewarding of all professions. Real teachers are inexhaustible and indispensable.

Teachers in Literature

And gladly wolde he lerne and gladly teche.–GEOFFREY CHAUCER

One good teacher in a lifetime may change a delinquent into a solid citizen.
–PHILIP WYLIE

Many a teacher is immortalized in literature. Teachers populate stories by Laura Ingalls Wilder (the *Little House* books), Muriel Spark (*The Prime of Miss Jean Brodie*), Belle Kaufman (*Up the Down Staircase*), John Knowles (*A Separate Peace*), and William Gibson (*The Miracle Worker*).

And cartoon teachers cavort across the television screen and comics pages—Geraldine Grundy (*Archie*), Miss Othmar (*Peanuts*), Edna Krabapple (*The Simpsons*), Les Moore (*Funky Winkerbean*), Miss Peach (*Miss Peach*), and Mr. Fogarty (*Luann*).

In her astonishing *Harry Potter* series, J. K. Rowling has resurrected the so-called school novel by creating a panorama of Hogwarts School faculty and staff. Charles Dickens would be proud of their whimsical names, among them Binns, Albus Dumbledore, Argus Filch, Filius Flitwick, Wilhelmina Grubbly-Plank, Madame Hooch, Gilderoy Lockhart, Remus Lupin, Minerva McGonagall, Madame Pince, Poppy Pomfrey, Quirinus Quirrell, Horace Slughorn, Severus Snape, Pomona Sprout, Sybill Trelawney, and (whew!) Dolores Umbridge.

Match each fictional teacher below with the author and literary work in which he or she lives:

1. Robert Anderson, *Tea and Sympathy* Mr. Antolini
2. Michael Chabon, *Wonderboys* George Caldwell
3. Joanna Cole, *The Magic School Bus* Arthur Chipping
4. Charles Dickens, *David Copperfield* Ichabod Crane
5. Charles Dickens, *Hard Times* Blanche DuBois
6. James Hilton, *Goodbye, Mr. Chips* Ms. Frizzle
7. Washington Irving, *The Legend of Sleepy Hollow* Thomas Gradgrind
8. Richard Llewellyn, *How Green Was My Valley* Mr. Gruffydd
9. J. D. Salinger, *The Catcher in the Rye* Henry Higgins
10. George Bernard Shaw, *Pygmalion* Mr. Mell
11. Tennessee Williams, *A Streetcar Named Desire* Bill Reynolds
12. John Updike, *The Centaur* Grady Tripp

Answers

1. Bill Reynolds 2. Grady Tripp 3. Ms. Frizzle 4. Mr. Mell 5. Thomas Gradgrind 6. Arthur Chipping

7. Ichabod Crane 8. Mr. Gruffydd 9. Mr. Antolini 10. Henry Higgins 11. Blanche DuBois 12. George Caldwell

Teacher Flicks

What we learn with pleasure we never forget.–ALFRED MERCIER

Good teaching is one-fourth preparation and three-fourths theater.
–GAIL GODWIN

"Nobody feels as good about what they do as you do."
–*MAD MEN* AD EXECUTIVE DON DRAPER
TO TEACHER SUZANNE FARRELL

Teaching may not be the most glamorous of professions, but teachers are featured in some of the most thoughtful and hilarious shows on television–from *Room 222* and *Welcome Back, Kotter* to *The Education of Max Bickford* and *Boston Public* to *Glee*.

Teachers have also inspired some of the most luminous and compelling films that Hollywood has produced. June Marlowe portrayed the comely Miss Crabtree in five *Little Rascals* films in the 1930s, and Robert Donat won an Oscar in 1939 for his depiction of the Mr. Chipping in *Goodbye, Mr. Chips*.

Focusing on more recent films, match the movies in the left-hand column with the actors in the right-hand column who portrayed the teachers, professors, or principals therein:

1. *How Green Was My Valley* (1941)   Anne Bancroft

2. *The Corn is Green* (1945)   Kathy Bates

3. *The Blackboard Jungle* (1955)   James Belushi

4. *The King and I* (1956)   Jack Black

5. *Tea and Sympathy* (1956)   Cate Blanchett

6. *The Miracle Worker* (1962)   Michael Caine

7. *Up the Down Staircase* (1967)   Russell Crowe

8. *To Sir, with Love* (1967)   Bette Davis

9. *The Prime of Miss Jean Brodie* (1969)   Sandy Dennis

10. *The Paper Chase* (1973)   Danny DeVito

11. *Conrack* (1974)   Michael Douglas

12. *Animal House* (1978)   Richard Dreyfus

13. *Fast Times at Ridgemont High* (1982)   Leif Erickson

14. *Class of 1984* (1982)   Tina Fey

15. *Educating Rita* (1983)   Albert Finney

16. *The Karate Kid* (1984)   Colin Firth

17. *Back to School* (1986)   Glenn Ford

18. *Ferris Bueller's Day Off* (1986)   Morgan Freeman

19. *Children of a Lesser God* (1986)   Mel Gibson

20. *The Principal* (1987)   Whoopi Goldberg

21. *Lean on Me* (1989)   Ryan Gosling

22. *Dead Poets Society* (1989)   John Houseman

23. *Stand and Deliver* (1989)   William Hurt

24. *Kindergarten Cop* (1990)   Deborah Kerr

25. *Sister Act II: Back in the Habit* (1993)   Sam Kinnison

26. *The Man Without a Face* (1993)   Kevin Kline

27. *Renaissance Man* (1994)   Roddy McDowall

28. *The Browning Version* (1994)   Pat Morita

29. *Mr. Holland's Opus* (1995)   Edward James Olmos

30. *Dangerous Minds* (1995)   Michelle Pfeiffer

31. *Good Will Hunting* (1997)   Walter Pigeon

32. *Rushmore* (1998)   Sidney Poitier

33. *Music of the Heart* (1999)   Alan Rickman

34. *Pay It Forward* (2000)   Julia Roberts

35. *Wonder Boys* (2000)   Arnold Schwarzenegger

36. *Harry Potter* film series (2001-2010)   Stellan Skarsgard

37. *A Beautiful Mind* (2001)   Maggie Smith

38. *The Emperor's Club* (2002)   Kevin Spacey

39. *Mona Lisa Smile* (2003)   Ben Stein

40. *School of Rock* (2003)   David Strathairn

41. *Mean Girls* (2004)   Meryl Streep

42. *Half Nelson* (2006)   Donald Sutherland

43. *Notes on a Scandal* (2006)   Hilary Swank

44. *Freedom Writers* (2006)   Jon Voight

45. *21* (2008)   Ray Walston

46. *Doubt* (2008)   Olivia Williams

47. *Blind Side* (2009)   Robin Williams

48. *A Single Man* (2009)

49. *An Education* (2009)

50. *Temple Grandin* (2010)

Answers

1. Walter Pigeon 2. Bette Davis 3. Glenn Ford 4. Deborah Kerr 5. Leif Erickson

6. Anne Bancroft 7. Sandy Dennis 8. Sidney Poitier (who also played a student in *The Blackboard Jungle*) 9. Maggie Smith 10. John Houseman

11. John Voight 12. Donald Sutherland 13. Ray Walston 14. Roddy McDowall 15. Michael Caine

16. Pat Morita 17. Sam Kinnison 18. Ben Stein 19. William Hurt 20. James Belushi

21. Morgan Freeman (playing real-life principal Joe Clark) 22. Robin Williams 23. Edward James Olmos (playing real-life teacher Jaime Escalante) 24. Arnold Schwarzenegger 25. Whoopi Goldberg 26. Mel Gibson 27. Danny DeVito 28. Albert Finney 29. Richard Dreyfus (who also played a professor in the TV series *The Education of Max Bickford*) 30. Michelle Pfeiffer (playing real-life teacher LouAnne Johnson)

31. Stellan Skarsgard 32. Olivia Williams 33. Meryl Streep (playing real-life teacher Roberta Guaspari) 34. Kevin Spacey 35. Michael Douglas

36. Alan Rickman 37. Russell Crowe 38. Kevin Klein 39. Julia Roberts 40. Jack Black

41. Tina Fey 42. Ryan Gosling. 43. Cate Blanchett 44. Hilary Swank (playing real-life teacher Erin Gruwell) 45. Kevin Spacey

46. Meryl Streep 47. Kathy Bates 48. Colin Firth 49. Olivia Williams 50. David Strathairn (playing real-life professor Carlock)

Famous School Reports–Characters

I had a terrible education.
I attended a school for emotionally disturbed teachers.
–WOODY ALLEN

There are advantages to being elected president.
The day after I was elected,
I had my high school grades classified Top Secret.
–RONALD REAGAN

- We may have to suspend Mary. She is quite contrary and keeps bringing that darned lamb to school.
- Georgie Porgie must stop kissing the girls and making them cry. I would like to see him play more with the boys, but Georgie just runs away from them.
- The Big Bad Wolf is exhibiting anti-social tendencies. He has already blown two houses down and devoured at least one grandmother.
- Jack shows great nimbleness and quickness in Physical Education. He is especially good at jumping over candlesticks.
- Humpty Dumpty had a great fall, but his grades and deportment deteriorated in the winter and spring. His boredom in the classroom has him climbing the walls, and his behavior has us all walking on eggshells.
- Pinocchio exhibits a lot of passive-aggressive behavior. Sometimes he is everybody's puppet. At other times, he sticks his big nose in everybody's business. We wooden kid you about that.

- We wish Atlas would show more joy at school. He acts like he has the weight of the world on his shoulders.

- We are impressed that the Cyclops has found the en-cyclops-pedia to be a real eye opener, but he just doesn't see eye to eye with his classmates. In fact, he causes us a lot of trouble for only one pupil.

- Narcissus appears to be too caught up in his own image. Yesterday he spent an hour staring at his reflection in the water in the boys' room toilet.

- Cain does not play well with others and has turned out to be a discipline problem. We have been willing to overlook some of his aggressive tendencies, but killing one quarter of the earth's population goes beyond what we are able to tolerate.

- After numerous requests, Samson finally got his hair cut, but he has been failing Physical Education ever since.

- Joshua is doing well in the horn section of the School Orchestra, but we can no longer tolerate his blowing down the walls.

- The Hulk has been a star heavyweight on the school wrestling team, but his classmates tease him for his tattered clothing and green complexion. To such criticism he does not react constructively. We recommend that he attend an anger-management class.

- Frankie Stein's antics in class keep us all in stitches, and many of his fellow students carry a torch for him. But, to be Frank, we are concerned that he may have a screw loose.

- Dracula can be a real pain in the neck and can get under our skin. At times, he acts like a spoiled bat and drives us batty. But the young count is a dedicated student. He stays up all night studying for his blood tests, and in mathematics class, his blood count is the highest. We predict that he will graduate Phi Batta Cape-a.

- The Mummy needs to learn to be more aware of the feelings of other pupils in the class. For now, he is too wrapped up in himself.

- The Invisible Boy often lies to avoid punishment, but we see right through him and find his fabrications to be quite transparent.

- Robinson Crusoe is to be commended for his dedication to completing his assignments. He always gets his homework done by Friday.

- Darth Vader is constantly upsetting his classmates and tends to look on the dark side of things. His habitual smoking in the boys' room is starting to affect his breathing and his voice.

- Being tall, dark, and hairy, King Kong thinks he has the girls in the palm of his hand. We wish he would break his habit of climbing up the school building.

- Hester Prynne is a straight-A student, but her classmates have pilloried her for her special abilities.

- Sherlock Holmes earns high grades in all subjects requiring deductive reasoning. In fact, he seems to know what questions we will ask on a test before he actually sees the test. As a result, he tends to find school elementary.

Famous Teacher Reports–People

Here is your child's progress report.
Sign the verification form at the top where indicated
and return to school with your child in the envelope.
–ACTUAL NOTE SENT HOME FROM SCHOOL

- In tense social situations, Marie Antoinette tends to lose her head. We recommend that she stop eating cake and go on a sugar-free diet.
- Jacky the Ripper has been tearing up the origami creations of his classmates.
- Having Tommy Edison in my class has been an illuminating experience. He is very bright, and when he gets an idea, a light bulb seems to go on above his head.
- Learned, knowledgeable, educated, studious, scholarly, well-informed, well-versed, and erudite Peter Roget demonstrates a far-ranging, comprehensive, inclusive, extensive, embracive, encompassing, exhaustive, encyclopedic, eclectic vocabulary. Moreover, he is a cooperative, collaborative, helpful, amenable, compliant, and symbiotic team player.
- Ludwig Van Beethoven behaves eccentrically in class. He hears music in his head but is not connected to an iPod. More seriously, all instructions from his teachers seem to fall on deaf ears.
- Michelangelo is continually finger-painting on the ceiling, and the custodial staff has incurred considerable expense to scrub away his drawings.

- Pablo Picasso exhibits possible talent in art, but he fails to show respect for authority For example, despite my instructions, he continues to draw both eyes on the same side of each head.
- Willie Shakespeare is failing Essay Writing because he refuses to write in prose, and his verse draws a blank with his classmates. If he continues in this matter, he will be Bard from the class.
- e. e. cummings is receiving low grades in Essay Writing primarily because of his lack of skill in the mechanics of composition. Despite my repeated requests, he refuses to use capital letters in his essays.
- Ptolemy needs to learn that the universe doesn't revolve around him.
- Jefferson Davis prefers to play with just a small number of his classmates and doesn't join in activities designed for the entire group. His fellow students have voted him Most Likely to Secede.
- Al Einstein is a problem child. He finds science and mathematics relatively easy, but he needs to pay more attention to his grooming.
- Marie Curie radiates enthusiasm in every project she undertakes.
- Do you have any suggestions about how we can break Ivan Pavlov of his annoying habit of drooling every time the school bell rings?
- Rodney Dangerfield always tries to be the class clown, but his classmates give him no respect.
- Although she cuts a fine figure, we had to suspend Tanya Harding because, in the playground, she keeps whacking her classmates in the knees. Due to such disruptive behavior, she is skating on thin ice.
- Tiger Woods is doing very well in golf class but failing Driver's Education. While he drives well on a fairway, he doesn't fare well on a driveway.
- Because of his bullying and other forms of anti-social behavior, we have had to place Al Capone in a very long detention period.
- Rodney King is to be commended for his cooperative spirit. He just wants everyone to get along.

- Although Bernie Madoff is creative with figures, he is getting a D in Mathematics because his numbers just don't add up. Nonetheless, we are pleased to report that Bernie has been elected Class Treasurer.

- As prom queen and captain of the cheerleading team, Sarah Palin is the most popular girl in the class. She is also an outstanding debater, able to refudiate all her opponents' arguments, and her peers have elected her president. But she is experiencing difficulty in Geography class, especially regarding the locations of Alaska and Russia.

Teachers' Advice to Students

There are obviously two educations.
One should teach us how to make a living and the other how to live.
–JAMES TRUSLOW ADAMS

The School Room

In September of 2005, Martha Cothren, a Social Studies teacher at Robinson High School in Little Rock, did something not to be forgotten.

On the first day of school, with the permission of the school superintendent, the principal, and the building supervisor, she removed all of the desks out of her classroom. When the first period kids entered the room, they discovered there were no desks. Looking around, confused, they asked, "Ms. Cothren, where are our desks?"

She replied, "You can't have a desk until you tell me what you have done to earn the right to sit at a desk."

They thought, "Well, maybe it's our grades."

"No," she said.

"Maybe it's our behavior."

She told them, "No, it's not even your behavior."

And so, they came and went through the first period, second period, third period, still with no desks in the classroom.

By early afternoon, television news crews had started gathering in Martha Cothren's classroom to report about this crazy teacher who had taken all of the desks out of her room. The final period of the day came and as the puzzled students found seats on the floor of the deskless classroom, Martha Cothren said, "Throughout the day, no one has been able to tell me just what he/she has done to earn the right to sit at the desks that are ordinarily found in this classroom. Now, I'm going to tell you."

At this point, Martha Cothren went over to the door of her classroom and opened it. Twenty-seven U.S. veterans, all in uniform, walked into the classroom. Each one was carrying a school desk. The vets began placing the school desks in rows, and then walked over to stand alongside the wall. By the time the last soldier had set the final desk in place, the kids started to understand, perhaps for the first time in their lives, just how the right to sit at those desks had been earned.

Martha said, "You didn't earn the right to sit at these desks. These heroes did it for you. They placed the desks here for you. Now, it's up to you to sit in them. It is your responsibility to learn, to be good students and to be good citizens. They paid the price so that you could have the freedom to get an education. Don't ever forget it."

A Teacher's In-Sight

Our teacher's husband unexpectedly died of a heart attack. About a week after his death, she shared some of her insight with us. As the late afternoon sunlight came streaming in through the classroom windows and the lesson was nearly over, she moved a few things aside on the edge of her desk and sat down there.

With a gentle look of reflection on her face, she paused and said, "Before class is over, I would like to share with all of you a thought that is unrelated to your studies, but what I feel is very important.

"Each of us is put here on earth to learn, share, love, appreciate, and give of ourselves. None of us knows when this fantastic experience will end. It can be taken away at any moment. Perhaps this is God's way of telling us that we must make the most out of every single day."

Her eyes beginning to water, she went on, "So I would like you all to make me a promise. From now on, as you go to school, or as you're heading home, find something beautiful to notice. It doesn't have to be something you see: It can be a scent, perhaps of freshly baked bread wafting out of someone's house, or it can be the sound of the breeze rustling the leaves in the trees, or the way the morning light catches one autumn leaf as it falls gently to the ground.

"Please look for these things, and cherish them. For, although it may sound trite to some, these things are the stuff of life. The little things we are put here on earth to enjoy. The things we often take for granted. We must make it important to notice them, for at any time it can all be taken away."

We were completely quiet as we picked up our books and filed out of the room silently. That afternoon, I noticed more things on my way home from school than I had that whole semester. Every once in a while, I think of that teacher and remember what an impression she made on all of us, and I try to appreciate all of those things that we sometimes overlook.

Take notice of something special you see on your lunch hour today. Go barefoot. Or walk on the beach at sunset. Stop off on the way home tonight to get a double-dip ice-cream cone. For as we get older, it is not the things we did that we often regret, but the things we didn't do.

Much Ado About "Nothing"

When a teacher retired after forty years in the classroom, there was a huge dinner for her. People flocked to the affair, not only colleagues and friends, but the numerous children, now grown to adulthood, whom she had taught over the years.

They spoke of the teacher's kindness, of her understanding, her sternness in the classroom coupled with her love of her students, and the special care she took to see to it that every student learned. Many of her former students attributed their success in later life to the values and knowledge they had learned as students in her classes.

Finally, it was the teacher's turn to speak, and as the master of ceremonies introduced her, he remarked that perhaps she would be willing to share some of the secrets of her success in teaching.

"There's no secret to it," she said as she began to speak. "On my first day of teaching, forty years ago, I walked into the classroom to find that my students had placed a tack on my chair, put an apple with a worm in it on my desk, and someone had written on the chalkboard, 'You can't teach us nothing!'

"Since that day, I have always checked my chair before sitting down, never eaten anything given to me by a student, and made it my special project to see to it that every child in my class learned.

"You see, within five minutes of that first day, I knew that my bottom could stand the tack and my stomach could survive the worm—but I realized that my conscience would never forgive me if I taught them 'nothing.'"

The Power of Good Words

In the few years I was a teacher I learned a lot of things. Perhaps the most important one of all was the glorious, life-changing power of an encouraging word. I discovered it early while I was still in college completing my student teaching hours in a local middle school.

I had read the work Leo Buscaglia had done with his University of Southern California students. In one exercise Leo and his students had made two lists of words, one positive and one negative. Then they had thrown the negative words in the trash and tried to use only the positive words for one month. They were amazed at how much better their lives became just by using words full of kindness and encouragement.

I decided to try this as well by finding something good to write on each paper my students handed in. It was a lot easier than I thought it would be. No matter how many errors a student's paper contained there was always a funny sentence, beautiful thought, or great idea that I could comment on. I remember glancing over my desk and seeing some of the students rereading those encouraging words again and again. It was a joy seeing their eyes shine a little brighter, their backs sit up a little straighter, and their learning climb a lot higher.

I recently saw one of my former students from that class, and we talked for a while. He was married, doing well in his job, and had two children of his own now. As I was saying goodbye, he said, "You know I still have a few of those old papers from your class. I still look at them from time to time. I just hope my kids have as good a teacher as you."

I walked off amazed at the effect those few positive words had on his life. I thanked God, too, for always giving me the words I needed as a teacher and as a writer. May your own life be forever full of encouraging words in your ears, from your lips, and in your heart.

–Joseph J. Mazzella

Classy Puns

A pun is the lowest form of wit.–JOHN DENNIS

If the pun is the lowest form of wit, it is, therefore, the foundation of all wit.
–HENRY ERSKINE

A pun is the lowest form of humor—if you don't think of it first.
–OSCAR LEVANT

Punning is largely the trick of compacting two or more ideas within a single word or phrase. Punning flouts the law of nature that pretends that two things cannot occupy the same space at the same time. Punning is an exercise of the mind at being concise. Punning is a rewording experience. Here's a line-up of puns designed to educate your mind about education. So, jest for the pun of it, let's get write to wit:

- My dog tried to eat my homework, but I took the words right out of its mouth.
- Extra-smart hamburgers and hot dogs end up on honor rolls.
- What is big and yellow and comes in the morning to brighten a mother's day?
  A school bus.
- What's furry, barks, and loves school?
  The teacher's pet.
- Who are the most popular boys in school?
  Art and Jim.
- Why are fish considered to be brain food?
  Because they travel in schools (and sometimes take debate).

- What's the difference between a student and a tightrope?
  One is taught, and the other is taut.
- Why is an English teacher like a strict judge?
  They both hand out long sentences.
- Why did Johnny walk backward to school?
  It was back-to-school day.
- What would you get if you crossed a school bully with a groundhog?
  Six more weeks of detention.
- Why is Alabama the smartest state in the nation?
  Because it has four As and a B.
- What's the difference between a conductor and a teacher?
  The conductor minds the train and a teacher trains the mind.
- What's the difference between a train and a teacher?
  A train goes "choo choo," and a teacher says, "Spit out your gum!"
- What's the difference between a fisherman and a lazy student?
  One baits his hooks, and the other hates his books.
- Where do boxers go to learn?
  The school of hard knocks.
- Why did the student carry a ladder to school?
  Because it was a high school.
- Why was the clock banned from the school library?
  Because it tocked too much.
- What is the fruitiest subject in school?
  History. It's full of dates.
- Why was the novel *Ivanhoe* banned from the school library?
  Because it contains too much Saxon violence.
- How many substitute teachers does it take to change a light-bulb?
  None. They just leave the room dark and show a movie.
- What did the math teacher say to the vampire?
  "Count, Dracula."
- Where do math teachers go to eat their midday meal?
  At the lunch counter.
- What is a math teacher's favorite animal?
  Adders.

- What kind of notebook grows on trees in the fall?
  Loose-leaf.
- Why would you want a magician to be sitting in a class with you?
  To help you solve the trick questions.
- Why do thermometers go to school?
  To earn their degrees.
- What is the best way to reduce pollution in schools?
  Use unleaded pencils.
- When is an exam not an exam?
  When you turn it into a teacher.
- Where do amphibian teachers work?
  In toad schools.
- Where was Sir Galahad educated?
  Knight school.
- What's the best place to eat ice cream?
  Sunday school.

Have You Heard?

One mark of a great educator is the ability
to lead students out to new places
where even the educator has never been.
–THOMAS GROOME

Have you heard about the music teacher? She joyfully makes her students face the music. She's fit as a fiddle and never blows her own horn and trumpets her achievements. She stays composed, never throws a tempo tantrum, and is always upbeat and up tempo. She sets the right tone in the classroom and strikes a responsive chord in each and every one of her students. She pulls out all the stops and never soft-pedals any of the high notes of music. She really can't be beat.

Have you heard about the mediocre student? He claims to get straight *A*s, but his *B*s, *C*s, and *D*s are curvy. His grades are like *America the Beautiful.* They go from *C* to shining *C.* Some of his grades are underwater. They're below *C* level. In fact, they're absolutely *D* grading. His grades are always lowest in January. He reasons that after Christmas everything is marked down.

And have you heard about . . .

- the cross-eyed teacher? *She couldn't control her pupils. (But she could control her students because they never knew when she was keeping an eye on them.)*
- the teacher who wore sunglasses in the classroom? *She had such bright students.*
- the teacher who tied all his students' shoelaces together? *They went on a class trip.*

- the music teacher who gave each of her students a small piece of paper? *She wanted to see if they could hold a note.*
- the teacher who came to class wearing a tuxedo? *He wanted to offer his students a formal education.*
- the teacher who had a crush on the head of the school? *She took out a loan with the bank, because she had interest in the principal.*
- the teacher who became a hero? *She stopped a kid napping.*
- the polite teacher? *He passed the nuts.*
- the math teacher who wanted to lose weight? *She gave up pi. When that didn't work, she decided to trinomials.*
- the science teacher who was involved in an automobile accident? *He was grading tests on a curve.*
- the science professor who taught astrophysics? *She pointed her students to pi in the sky.*
- the history teacher who became a contestant on a popular TV show? *It's called* The Dating Game.
- the professor who revised her syllabus to reveal the crucial role that women play in shaping world events? *She changed the course of history.*
- the algebra teacher? *She was an agent of math instruction.*
- the woman who trained an aged antelope to bark? *She proved that you* can *teach an old gnu dog tricks.*
- the cannibal who attended high school? *He kept buttering up his teacher.*
- the high school girl who was the valedictorian of her class and was also the prom queen? *It's actually not that impressive—she was home-schooled.*
- the student who flunked his vocabulary test? *Words failed him.*
- the student who brought her math homework to gym class? *She wanted to work out her problems.*
- the student who bungee-jumped off the roof of the schoolhouse? *He was suspended.*
- the student who always did her homework on airplanes? *She wanted a higher education.*
- the elf student? *He had a lot of gnomework.*
- the witch student? *She earned an* A *in spelling.*

- the student who studied hard for his apiary exam? *He got a bee.*
- the ghost that haunted the classroom? *It was a source of school spirit.*
- the giraffe student? *It had the highest marks.*
- the seal that got only average grades? *It was a C-lion.*
- the dog that couldn't get into obedience school? *It had low S.I.T. scores.*
- the cat who became valedictorian of her class? *She got purr-fect grades on all her tests.*
- the young whale that was sent to the principal's office? *It was punished for spouting off at the teacher, so it started blubbering.*
- the school for arachnids? *They learn reeling, writhing, and a rhythmic tick.*
- the insect that earned an *A* in English class? *It was a spelling bee.*
- the snake that flunked out of school? *It couldn't raise its hand to answer the teachers' questions.*
- the centipede that was late for school? *That morning its mother had played "This little piggy goes to market" with it. Then it took the insect another hour to put on its galoshes.*

Why I Flunked Out of High School

I was thrown out of college for cheating on the metaphysics exam.
I looked into the soul of the boy next to me.
–WOODY ALLEN

Any day that you had gym was a weird school day.
It started out normal—English, geometry, social studies
—and then suddenly you're in Lord of the Flies *for forty minutes.*
You're hanging from a rope; you hardly have any clothes on.
Kids are throwing dodgeballs at you, snapping towels. . . .
And then it's history, science, language.
There's something off in the whole flow of that day.
–JERRY SEINFELD

In English class, I went through a bad spell, and I kept misplacing my modifiers and dangling my participles in public. When I was presented with oral quizzes in vocabulary, fear took the words out of my mouth. And my writing made me feel as if I was serving a life sentence.

In History class, I had no remembrance of things past because I couldn't see any future in studying the subject. On tests, I made one error for each era.

Math class did a number on me. As the term progressed, I became number and number. My angles were never right. They were never acute and always obtuse. I couldn't even add, so I turned out to be a total failure.

In Computer Science, I developed a terminal illness and lost my memory. I lost my drive and flunked my screen test—and the course. I experienced vial reactions to Chemistry. The subject and I just didn't have any chemistry. I had no formula for success, so I couldn't master the elements of the subject. The acid test and the litmus test are that I couldn't come up with any solutions.

In foreign language classes, I got lost in translation. I wasn't a Latin lover, and the teacher had to pardon my French because it was all Greek to me.

I failed Art because the subject didn't suit my pallet, so I drew a blank.

I went out for the School Orchestra, but I was so high-strung and keyed up that I didn't know how to conduct myself. I fiddled around so much that the teacher wouldn't let me play even second fiddle. It was all too much sax and violins for me, so I played everything by ear and gave a second-string performance. My failure was noteworthy, and my flatter E got me nowhere.

I found the lines too long for Drama class, so I couldn't get by the first stage of the course. I never got my act together, and the teacher told me I was a bad actor. I even tried being a stagehand, but I soon needed a change of scenery.

Wood Shop was boring, and I couldn't do the drill. The subject went against my grain, so I didn't make the cut.

I was all charged up to take Electric Shop, but I had a negative experience in that class. I wasn't very bright, and I wasn't able to stay current. The teacher found my performance to be shocking and re-volting but never electrifying. The light bulb above my head never lit up.

Home Economics. Well, to be honest, I couldn't boil water without burning it. My cooking just didn't pan out, my cakes and pies were half baked, and, ultimately, my goose was cooked.

In Driver's Ed., I thought I was in the driver's seat. I was placed in an accelerated course, but I was all over the road. I thought I got bad brakes, but the instructor told me I was shiftless, no good in the clutch, and couldn't get it in gear.

In Phys. Ed. I just wasn't fit for the class, and I wasn't up to speed. I couldn't learn the ropes, but I did climb the walls. I didn't shape up, so I was shipped out.

I even flunked homeroom. I wasn't exactly the class clown, but I was the class trapeze artist. I was always getting suspended.

Animal Cracker Uppers

Dr. Porter visited the school and lectured on "Destructive Pests."
A large number were present.
—ACTUAL NEWS STORY

Functional Canine

An elementary school teacher was delivering a station wagon full of kids home one day when a fire truck zoomed past. Sitting in the front seat of the truck was a Dalmatian. The children started discussing the dog's duties.

"They use him to keep crowds back," said one child.

"No," said another, "he's just for good luck."

A third child brought the argument to a close: "They use the dogs," she said firmly, "to find the fire hydrants."

Pig Tale

A first-grade teacher was reading the story of "The Three Little Pigs" to her class. She came to the part where the first pig was trying to gather the building materials for his home: "And so the pig went up to the man with the wheelbarrow full of straw and said, 'Pardon me, sir, but may I have some of that straw to build my house?'" The teacher paused then asked the class, "And what do you think that man said?"

One little boy raised his hand and opined, "I think he said, 'Wow! A talking pig!'"

Cat Tale

A kindergarten pupil told her teacher that she had found a cat, but it was dead. "How did you know that the cat was dead?" the teacher asked.

"I pissed in its ear, and it didn't move."

"You did WHAT?

"You know. I leaned over and went *Pssst!* and it didn't move."

The Sounds of Learning

A group of children were sitting in a circle with their teacher. She was going around in turn asking them all questions:

"Davy, what noise does a cow make?"

"It goes *moo*, Miss."

"Alice, what noise does a cat make?"

"It goes *meow*, Miss."

"Jamie, what noise does a lamb make?"

"It goes *baaa*, Miss."

"Jennifer, what noise does a mouse make?"

"It goes . . . *click!*"

Botany Lesson

The teacher was telling the class about plants that have the word *dog* in front of their names—*dogrose, dogwood, dog violet,* and the like.

She asked the class if they could name another flower with the prefix *dog*.

Steven raised his hand and said, "Sure, Miss Jones, a collie flower!"

The Dopey Little Puppy

A seven-year-old girl came into the school library to sign out a puppy-training DVD. DVDs usually check out for a week, so the librarian was surprised when the girl brought back the DVD the next day. "How did the puppy-training DVD work out for you?" the librarian asked the girl.

"Oh, not very well," she replied. "I couldn't get him to watch it for very long. At his age, he's mostly interested in food, you know."

Barking Up the Wrong Tree

"Sam, what is the outside of a tree called?" asked the teacher.

"I don't know."

"Bark, Sam, bark."

"Bow wow!"

Overconfidence

It was the end of the school year, and a kindergarten teacher was receiving gifts from her pupils.

The florist's son handed her a gift. She shook it, held it overhead, and said, "I bet I know what it is. Flowers."

"That's right!" the boy exclaimed. "But, how did you know?"

"Oh, just a wild guess," the teacher said.

The next pupil was the sweet shop owner's daughter. The teacher held her gift overhead, shook it, and said, "I bet I can guess what it is. A box of sweets."

"That's right, but how did you know?" asked the girl.

"Oh, just a wild guess," said the teacher.

The next gift was from the son of the liquor store owner. The teacher held the package overhead, but it was leaking onto her dress.

"Is it wine?" she asked.

"No," the boy replied, with some excitement.

"Is it champagne?" the teacher asked.

"No," the boy replied, with more excitement.

"I give up, what is it?"

With great glee, the boy replied, "It's a puppy!"

A Teacher's Covenant

Teaching is not a lost art, but the regard for it is a lost tradition.
–JACQUES BARZUN

Teachers are expected to reach unattainable goals with inadequate tools. The miracle is that at times they accomplish this impossible task.
–HAIM G. GINOTT

L et me see if I've got this right. You want me to go into that room with all those kids, and fill their every waking moment with a love for learning.

You want me for the safety, inspiration, and academic growth of up to thirty-six individuals at once up to seven hours at a stretch. And you want me to be "on" every minute of those hours?

Not only that, I'm to instill a sense of pride in their ethnicity, modify disruptive behavior, and observe them for signs of abuse.

I am to fight racism, the war on drugs and sexually transmitted diseases, check their backpacks for guns, and raise their self-esteem.

I am to teach my students good citizenship, sportsmanship, and fair play, how and where to register to vote, how to balance a checkbook, and how to apply for a job.

I am responsible for anything that happens to any of my students in my classroom. I am responsible for their safety and their health. I am to check their heads occasionally for lice, maintain a safe environment, recognize signs of potential anti-social behavior, offer advice, write letters of recommendation for student employment and scholarships, encourage a respect for the cultural diversity of others, and, oh yeah, teach—always making sure that I give the girls in my class fifty percent of my attention.

I am required by my contract to be working on my own time (summers and evenings) and at my own expense toward advanced certification and to sponsor the cheerleaders and the sophomore class after school.

I am to attend committee and faculty meetings and participate in staff development training to maintain my current certification and employment status.

I am to purchase supplies, room decorations, bulletin board supplies, for children who can't afford them, and luxury items such as scissors, glue, scotch tape, paper clips, notebook paper, red pens, and markers with my own money as there is no money in the budget for these items.

I am to do all of this with just a piece of chalk, a few books, and a bulletin board, and on a starting salary that qualifies my family for food stamps in many states. Is that all?

The Answering Machine at School

Hello! You have reached the automated answering service of your school. In order to assist you in connecting the right staff member, please listen to all your options before making a selection:

- To lie about why your child is absent - *Press 1.*
- To make excuses for why your child did not do his work - *Press 2.*
- To complain about what we do - *Press 3.*
- To cuss out staff members - *Press 4.*
- To ask why you didn't get information that was already in your newsletter and several flyers mailed to you - *Press 5.*
- If you want us to raise your child - *Press 6.*
- If you want to reach out and touch, slap, or hit someone - *Press 7.*
- To request another teacher for the third time this year - *Press 8.*
- To complain about bus transportation - *Press 9.*
- To complain about school lunches - *Press 0.*

If you realize that this is the real world and your child must be responsible and accountable for his or her behavior and schoolwork, please hang up and have a nice day!

Short Takes

I am still learning–MICHELANGELO

I was still learning when I taught my last class.–CLAUDE FUESS

I am learning all the time. The tombstone will be my diploma.
–EARTHA KITT

A Noteworthy Message
A wise schoolteacher sent this note to all parents on the first day of school: "If you promise not to believe everything your child says happens at school, I'll promise not to believe everything they say happens at home."

Brownie Points
Teacher: Where is your homework?

Student: I lost it fighting this kid who said you weren't the best teacher in the school.

An Educational Journey
When I was a boy, I walked ten miles to school every day, sometimes in the rain or snow. Man, did I feel stupid when I found out there was a bus.

Cafeteria Food
When the power went off at the elementary school, the cook couldn't serve a hot meal in the cafeteria. She had to feed the children something, so at the last minute she whipped up great stacks of peanut butter and jelly sandwiches. As one little boy filled his plate, he said, "It's about time. At last—a home cooked meal!"

On a Toot!
A tutor who tutored the flute
Tried to tutor two tooters to toot.
     Said the two to the tutor,
     "Is it easier to toot or
"To tutor two tooters to toot?"

Department Chairs
Two old men, one a retired professor of psychology and the other a retired professor of history, were sitting on the porch of a retirement home, watching the sun set. The professor of history said to the professor of psychology, "Have you read Marx?"

To which the professor of psychology said, "Yes, I think it's the wicker chairs."

Making the Grade
On one occasion, a student burst into his professor's office: "Sir, I don't believe I deserve this F you've given me."

To which the professor replied, "I agree, but unfortunately it's the lowest grade the university will allow me to give."

Book It!
A clueless freshman was in his college campus bookstore. When he asked the store clerk about a book for one of his classes, the fellow responded, "This book will do half the job for you."

"Good," the freshman replied. "I'll take two."

Whither History?
At a parent information night held at high school, one father in the audience raised his hand. "I haven't heard one word about history tonight," he lamented. "Has history become a thing of the past?"

Whew!
Boy: Isn't the principal a dummy!
Girl: Say, do you know who I am?
Boy: No.
Girl: I'm the principal's daughter.
Boy: And do you know who I am?
Girl: No.
Boy: Thank goodness!

In a Quandary

While marking her pupils' Social Studies test papers, the teacher was in a quandary about the answer given by one of the third-graders. Asked to name the four major directions, he wrote:

1. Listen carefully.
2. Write neatly.
3. Sit up straight.
4. Raise your hand.

Vegging Out

Teacher: What is the Gross National Product?
Student: Broccoli.

The Teacher Detective

Teacher: Seymour, you copied from Susan's test, didn't you?
Student: How did you find out?
Teacher: Susan's test answer says, "I don't know," and yours says, "Me neither."

Schoolishness

*Remember in elementary school, you were told that in case of fire
you have to line up quietly in a single file line from smallest to tallest.
What is the logic in that? What, do tall people burn slower?*
–WARREN HUTCHERSON

*More high schools are cutting out gym classes to make room
for increased requirements in math and science.
So now when kids get fat and fall down,
they'll at least know the science behind it.*
–JAY LENO

Heavenly Teachers

Three people knocked on the gates of Heaven. St. Peter asked,
"Who's there?"

"It's me, Sally Smith," the voice replied. St. Peter let her in.

"It's me, Jimmy Jones," said the second. St. Peter let him in.

"It is *I,* Verla Vilas," answered the third.

"Excellent," smiled St. Peter. "An English teacher!"

St. Peter welcomed the teacher into Heaven and told her he would
give her a special tour of where she would reside for eternity.

The first neighborhood was lovely—exquisite mansions set in gorgeous grounds. The teacher asked if this is where she would live, but
St. Peter said it was just for lawyers. The teacher rolled her eyes and
sighed.

They floated on, and the teacher saw another neighborhood that
was even more beautiful. The mansions were even more lavish. People
strolled park lawns, socialized, and played golf on a beautiful course.
Everyone was having a terrific time. Again she inquired if this is where
she would live, but St. Peter said it was just for doctors. Again her eyes
rolled.

On through the clouds they drifted and soon came to a third neighborhood. It was the most luminous of all. Added to the grandest mansions, parks, pools, and golf courses were magnificent libraries, schools, theaters, and concert halls. St. Peter told the teacher this would be her new home in Heaven. The teacher was thrilled, but she noticed that no one was around, and all the mansions seemed to be empty.

She asked St. Peter where everyone was. Don't many teachers make it to Heaven? St. Peter announced that yes, there were lots of teachers in Heaven, but they wouldn't return until the next day. They were all in Hell attending an in-service training session.

Making the Grade I

A seventeen-year-old girl had just gotten her driver's license and offered to take her mom's car to the gas station. She pulled up to the full-service pumps, and the attendant asked, "What grade, miss?"

"Eleventh!" she replied.

Making the Grade II

A schoolteacher expecting her first child attended natural childbirth classes. When she went to the hospital in labor, she found that one of her classmates had also arrived and was also in labor. The classmate immediately requested drugs to ease her pain, while the teacher gave birth aided only by her husband's coaching.

When the nurses rolled the teacher out of the delivery room, she spotted a chalkboard. Beside her classmate's name was an A-; next to hers was a B+.

"Honey, look at that!" the teacher complained to her husband. "She took all the drugs they gave her and made an A-. I gave birth naturally and only got a B+."

Her patient husband rolled his eyes. "Sweetheart," he said, "that's your blood type."

A Matter of Principal

On the first day of school, the principal made his rounds and heard a terrible commotion coming from one of the classrooms. He rushed in and spotted one young man, much taller than the others, who seemed to be making the most noise. He seized the lad, dragged him to the hall, and told him to wait there until he was excused.

Returning to the classroom, the principal restored order and lectured the class for half an hour about the importance of good behavior.

When he was finished, he said, "Now, are there any questions?"

One girl stood up timidly and said, "Please, sir, may we have our teacher back?"

Oldest Excuse in the Book

"Johnny, where's your homework?" the teacher asked the little boy while holding out her hand.

"My dog ate it," Johnny answered.

"Johnny, I've been a teacher for eighteen years. Do you really expect me to believe that?"

"It's true, Miss Tanner, I swear," insisted the boy. "I had to force him, but he ate it!"

Iron Man

A high school teacher injured his back and had to wear a plaster cast around the upper part of his body. It fit under his shirt and wasn't noticeable.

On the first day of the term, still with the cast under his shirt, the teacher found himself assigned to the toughest students in the school. Walking confidently into the rowdy classroom, he opened the window as wide as possible and then busied himself with paperwork at his desk.

When a strong breeze made his tie flap, he picked up the stapler from his desk and stapled his tie to his chest. After that, he had no discipline problems with any of his students that term.

Turning the Tables

In the traffic court of a large midwestern city, a young woman was brought before the judge to answer for a ticket she received for driving through a red light. She explained to the judge that she was a schoolteacher and requested an immediate disposal of her case so she could get to the school on time.

A wild gleam came into the judge's eyes. "You're a schoolteacher, eh?" he said. "Madam, I shall realize my lifelong ambition. I've waited years to have a schoolteacher in this court. Now sit down at that table and write 'I will not drive through red lights' five hundred times!"

Production Line

The teacher of a high school class in the fundamentals of economics led the discussion around to the population explosion. "Certain levels of our society reproduce much more frequently than others," he pointed out. "What people would you guess reproduce the most?"

One bright student answered, "Women?"

American Signing Language

A little boy just couldn't seem to learn. One day his teacher asked him who signed the Declaration of Independence. He didn't know. For almost a week she asked him the same question every day, but still he couldn't come up with the right answer.

Finally, in desperation, she called the boy's father to her office. "Your boy won't tell me who signed the Declaration of Independence," she lamented.

"Come here, son, and sit down," the dad said to the boy. "Now if you signed that crazy thing, just admit it so we can get out of here!"

Gotcha!

At a prestigious southern university, there were four sophomores taking Organic Chemistry. They did so well on all the quizzes, midterms, and labs that each had an *A* for the semester.

These four friends were so confident that the weekend before finals, they decided to drive up to Charlottesville to the University of Virginia and party with some friends up there. They had a great time, but, after all the hard partying, they slept all day Sunday and didn't make it back to their university until early Monday morning.

Rather than taking the final then, they decided to find their professor later and explain to him why they missed taking the test. They reported that they had gone to UVA for the weekend with the plan to come back in time to study, but, unfortunately, they had a flat tire on the way back, didn't have a spare, and couldn't get help for a long time. As a result, they missed the examination.

The professor thought it over and then agreed they could make up the final the following day. The students were relieved and elated. They studied that night and went in the next day at the time the professor had told them. He placed them in separate rooms, handed each of them a test booklet, and told them to begin. They looked at the first problem, worth five points, something simple about free radical formation.

"Cool," each one thought at the same time, each one in his separate room. "This is going to be easy." Each finished the problem and then turned the page.

On the second page was written (for ninety-five points): "Which tire was flat?"

A Remarkable School

Meant-To has a friend. His name is Didn't-Do. Have you met them?
They live together in a house called Never-Win.
I am told it is haunted by the ghost of Might-Have-Been.
–MARVA COLLINS

Don't try to fix the students. Fix ourselves first.
The good teacher makes the poor student good and the good student superior.
When our students fail, we, as teachers, too, have failed.
–MARVA COLLINS

Inspired by the vision of educator Marva Collins, the Marva Collins Preparatory School of Wisconsin, in Milwaukee, is an institution of uncompromising academic and social expectations for inner-city children, grades K-8. The school offers a rigorous, values-based curriculum and an unconditional love of and trust in the students.

Among the students, almost 100% are African American, 87% qualify for free or reduced-cost lunch, and more than 75% come from single-parent homes. Children are admitted on a random-selection basis, and are nurtured by Marva Collins's philosophy that all children can learn and there is no excuse for academic underachievement by ghetto children. The Marva Collins creed announces, "I will let society predict, but only I can determine what I will, can or cannot do." Mrs. Collins asserts that "Children don't fail; teachers do," and MCPS takes as its responsibility to ensure that every child succeeds.

The school offers a demanding core curriculum of phonics, reading, poetry, vocabulary, foreign language, and mathematics. When I (the author of this book) visited the school in 2008, I noted that the fifth- through eighth graders with whom I worked were already studying Latin and versions of Shakespeare's *Hamlet* and *Julius Caesar*, and when I performed some spoonerized stories for them, they knew what a spoonerism was. In addition, students are urged to enroll in co-curricular activities such as ballet, drama, chess, music, art, and tae kwon do.

Each student at Marva Collins Prep is asked to write a mission statement about his or her goals in life. As a concrete example of the level of work in this remarkable Milwaukee school, I offer the mission statement of fifth-grader Marcus Jenkins:

"My mission in life is to become a successful neurosurgeon like Dr. Ben Carson. I recently read *Gifted Hands* by Dr. Carson, and the book inspired me to want to be just like him. He has the abilities to save children's lives and he persevered in spite of everything that happened to him when he was growing up. Dr. Ben Carson is a true leader who takes pride in his work.

"'People with goals succeed because they know where they are going.' This proverb helps me to stay focused and think about what I want to do when I become an adult. Even though I am very young, just knowing that there are people out there who were once young boys full of hope for the future, just like me, makes me want to become someone very, very special, just like Dr. Ben Carson."

Since it opened its door in 1997, Marva Collins Preparatory School has increased its enrollment sixfold, with a waiting list of more than a hundred. During my visit, I saw how powerfully the school had opened not just doors, but minds. As Marva Collins principal Robb Raugh says, "MCPS imparts an indisputable quality to each student: you are special, you are competent, you are capable. Years from now, that value system will be every bit as important as the quantitative scores we measure today."

We feel the strength of self-image in a statement from fourth-grader Jade Robertson: "I believe that I am special. I love myself even if nobody else does. I respect myself for being who I am. I know whatever I'm doing, I'm going to aim one degree higher."

Language Arts

We teach who we are.–JOHN GARDNER

English teachers are novel lovers. They remind us that books were the original laptops. They inspire us to read POETRY and to TRY POE. They help us to go from Bard to verse.

Nostalgic Grammar teachers find the past perfect and the present tense. They help us to avoid Post Grammatic Stress Syndrome. They undangle our participles and unsplit our infinitives and show us how to write right. And old Grammar teachers never die. They just lose their verb and slip into a comma—but they gain great re-noun in their students' memory.

Because of our affection for English teachers, we make up jokes about language arts classrooms:

Letter Imperfect
An English teacher often wrote comments on her students' essays. She was working late one night, and as the hours passed, her hand-writing deteriorated.

The next day a student came to her after class with his essay she had corrected. "I can't make out this comment you wrote on my paper."

The teacher took the paper, and after squinting at it for a minute, sheepishly replied, "It says that you need to write more legibly."

Forbidden Words
Another English teacher announced to the class: "There are two words I simply don't allow in my class. One is *gross* and the other is *cool*."

From the back of the room a voice called out, "So, what are the words?"

Marks Make a Difference

And another English teacher wrote on the board "Woman without her man is nothing" and instructed his students to punctuate the sentence.

The males in the class wrote: "Woman, without her man, is nothing."

The females wrote: "Woman! Without her, man is nothing!"

Positively Positive

A linguistics professor was lecturing to his class one day. "In English," he said, "a double negative forms a positive. In some languages though, such as Russian, a double negative is still a negative. However," he pointed out, "there is no language wherein a double positive can form a negative."

A voice from the back of the room piped up, "Yeah, sure."

Eyes on the Prize

During an English lesson, the teacher called on Bobby to recite a sentence with a direct object. Bobby thought and said, "Teacher, everybody thinks you are beautiful."

"Why thank you, Bobby," the teacher said, blushing. "But what is the direct object?"

"A good grade on my report card," he replied.

Grammar Stammer

Teacher: Ellen, give me a sentence starting with *I*.

Ellen: I is . . .

Teacher: No, Ellen. Always say, "I am . . . "

Ellen: All right, . . . *I* am the ninth letter of the alphabet.

Lucky Guess

Teacher: Billy, name two pronouns.

Billy: Who me?

Teacher: Correct!

Grammar with Conviction

Teacher: Give an example of a compound sentence.

Student: If a man was forced to serve two prison terms.

A Passion for Grammar

An English teacher spent a lot of time marking grammatical errors in her students' written work. She wasn't sure how much impact she was having until one overly busy day when she sat at her desk rubbing her temples.

A student asked, "What's the matter, Mrs. Sheridan?"

"Tense," she replied, describing her emotional state.

After a slight pause the student tried again. "What was the matter? What has been the matter? What might have been the matter?"

In the Wrong Mood

Teacher: Analyze this sentence: "It was getting to be milking time." What mood?

Student: The cows.

Give Me a Sign

Mom and Dad took their first-grade son on a car trip to Canada. To help pass the time, the boy practiced his new reading skills by calling out road signs.

He fell asleep just before they entered Quebec. When he awoke, he saw the French highway signs and moaned loudly, "While I was asleep I forgot how to read!"

Building Better Vocabularies

*He who graduates today and stops learning tomorrow
is uneducated the day after.*
–NEWTON BAKER

When you're through learning, you're through.–VERNON LAW

Undistinguished Writing

Yale University professor William Lyon Phelps found this gem gleaming out of a student essay: "The girl tumbled down the stairs and lay prostitute at the bottom."

In the margin of the paper Phelps commented: "My dear young man: You must learn to distinguish between a fallen woman and one who has merely slipped."

A Word for Life

Stressing the importance of a good vocabulary, the teacher told her young charges, "Use a word ten times, and it shall be yours for life."

From somewhere in the back of the room, came a male voice chanting, "Amanda, Amanda, Amanda, Amanda, Amanda, Amanda, Amanda, Amanda, Amanda, Amanda."

A Triple Play

Teacher: Use *deduct, defense,* and *detail* in a sentence.

Student: Deduct waddled across the field, and defeat went over defense before detail.

Out of Context I

Teacher: Use the word *mention* in a sentence.

Student: In *Tarzan of the Apes*, the apes had to mention baby Tarzan.

Teacher: I don't understand your sentence.

Student: But doesn't *mention* mean "bring up"?

Out of Context II

A student wrote the following sentence in an essay: "The fireman came down the ladder pregnant."

The teacher took the girl aside to correct her. "Don't you know what *pregnant* means?" she asked.

"Sure," said the student confidently, "It means 'carrying a child.'"

Out of Context II

Teacher: Use the word *cliché* in a sentence.

Student: The boy came into the classroom from recess with a cliché on his face.

Teacher: But that's not how we use the word *cliché*.

Student: Why not? A cliché is "a worn out expression."

Unattractive Opposites

An English teacher was giving a lesson on writing about emotions. First he asked, "Now then, what is the opposite of sadness?"

"*Joy*," replied one of the students.

"And the opposite of *depression*?"

"*Elation*," said another.

"And what is the opposite of *woe*?"

"I believe that would be *giddy-up*."

34

Under a Spell

You know there's a problem with the education system
when you realize that out of the three Rs only one begins with an R.
–DENNIS MILLER

It took me five years to learn how to spell Chattanooga.
Then we moved to Albuquerque.
–JOE MORRISON

On the A List
Teacher: What letter comes after *A* in the alphabet?
Student: All of them.

Agri-Culture
Teacher: "How do you spell *farm*?"
Student: "Let me think. 'Old McDonald had a farm.' Okay, the answer is E-I-E-I-O."

Hole Language
Teacher: "If *can't* is a contraction of *cannot* and *won't* is a contraction of *will not*, what is *don't* a contraction of?
Student: Donut?

In a State
Summer vacation was over and the teacher asked little Emily about her family trip.

"We visited my grandmother in Minneapolis, Minnesota."

The teacher asked, "Good, can you tell the class how you spell that?"

After careful thought, Emily said, "Actually, we went to Maine."

Letter Perfect
The teacher of a first-grade class gave a trivia quiz for fun. If the child got the right answer, he or she got a sticker. One question was "What is the capital of Washington?"

A young boy raised his hand excitedly and volunteered that the capital of Washington is *W*.

Naturally the teacher gave him a sticker.

The Sound of Silence
The second-grade teacher asked little Mollie how to spell the word *knit*.

Molly said, "*n-i-t*."

"No, try again."

Molly said, very slowly, "*n-i-t*."

Finally the teacher told Molly the correct spelling, "*k-n-i-t*."

Molly looked at the teacher, hands on hips, and huffed, "But you said *k* is silent."

Write On!
Said a boy to his teacher one day,
"*Wright*'s not written *rite*, I would say."
So the teacher replied,
As the error she eyed,
"Right. *Wright*. Write *rite* right, right away."

Honesty
Teacher: Glenn, how do you spell *crocodile*?

Student: K-r-o-k-o-d-i-a-l.

Teacher: No, that's wrong

Student: Maybe it's wrong, but you asked me how I spell it.

A Grave Misspelling

Teacher: How do you spell *coffin?*
Little Dracula: K-a-u-g-h-i-n-n.
Teacher: That's the worst *coffin* spell I have ever heard.

So Far, So Good

Teacher: Your spelling is much better, Ronald. Only five mistakes that time.
Student: Thank you, Mrs. Smith.
Teacher: Now let's go on to the next word.

A Formula for Good Spelling

Teacher: Spell *water.*
Student: H-i-j-k-l-m-n-o.
Teacher: That doesn't spell *water.*
Student: Yes, it does. It's all the letters from *H* to *O.*

A Ginormous Misunderstanding

Jake was six and learning to read. He pointed at a picture in a zoo book and said to his teacher, "Look! It's a frickin' elephant!"

Deep breath . . . "What did you call it?"

"It's a frickin' elephant! It says so on the picture!"

And so it did: African Elephant.

Intra Murals

Teacher: Why did cavemen draw pictures of rhinoceroses, hippopotamuses, and pterodactyls on the walls of their caves?

Student: Because they weren't able to spell the names.

The Most Unhappy Speller

"I've just had the most awful time," said a boy to his friends. "First I got angina pectoris, then arteriosclerosis. Just as I was recovering, I got psoriasis. They gave me hypodermics, and to top it all, tonsillitis was followed by appendectomy."

"Wow! How did you pull through?" sympathized his friends.

"I don't know," the boy replied. "That was the toughest spelling test I ever had."

A (Don)Key Distinction

A college professor received a composition in which one of his students enthusiastically described his adventures in Venezuela, where he had worked the previous summer. One error kept appearing throughout the narrative: The student consistently misspelled the word *burro* as *burrow*.

Seizing the delicious opportunity, the professor wrote at the end of the essay, "I thoroughly enjoyed your enthusiastic narrative about your adventures in Venezuela and your love of its fauna. But it is apparent to me from your spelling that you do not know your ass from a hole in the ground."

Payment Plan

In a message to its parents, a famous private school omitted a key letter from a key word: "Due to rising costs, we shall have to increase our tuition to $10,850 per anum."

An irate father wrote back to the school to complain, "I'd much rather pay through the nose!"

35

Proverbial Wisdom

By learning you will teach, by teaching you will learn.
–LATIN PROVERB

A teacher is better than two books.
–GERMAN PROVERB

He who is afraid of asking is ashamed of learning.
–DANISH PROVERB

Do not confine your children to your own learning,
for they were born in another time.
–HEBREW PROVERB

When the pupil is ready, the teacher will come.
–CHINESE PROVERB

Teachers open the door, but you must enter yourself.
–CHINESE PROVERB

A first-grade teacher collected well-known proverbs. She gave her students the first half of a proverb and asked them to write the ending. Here's what they came up with:

- Strike while the . . . bug is close.
- Where there's smoke, there's . . . pollution.
- You get out of something what you . . . see pictured on the box.
- Don't bite the hand that . . . looks dirty.
- Never underestimate the power of . . . termites.
- When the blind lead the blind . . . get out of the way.
- If you lie down with dogs . . . you will stink in the morning.

- It's always darkest before . . . daylight savings time.
- There are none so blind as . . . Stevie Wonder.
- If at first you don't succeed . . . get new batteries.
- Laugh and the world laughs with you. Cry and . . . you have to blow your nose.
- A miss is as good as a . . . Mr.
- Children should be seen and not . . . spanked or grounded.
- A penny saved is . . . not much.
- An idle mind is . . .the best way to relax.
- As you shall make your bed so shall you . . . mess it up.
- Better be safe than . . . punch a fifth grader.
- You can lead a horse to water but . . . how?
- You can't teach an old dog new . . . math.
- Two's company. Three's . . . the Musketeers.
- No news is . . . impossible.
- Love all, trust . . . me.
- Don't put off tomorrow . . . what you put on to go to bed.
- The pen is mightier than the . . . pigs.
- A bird in the hand . . . is going to poop on you.

36

Science Friction

The work can wait while you show the child the rainbow,
but the rainbow won't wait while you do the work.
–PATRICIA CLAFFORD

I'd rather read a sixth grader's composition on butterflies
written after watching a monarch chrysalis in a field of milkweed
than view a multimedia display referencing the latest entomological
research downloaded from the Internet.
–CLIFFORD SCOTT

We always have good chemistry with science teachers. They help us to come up with the right solutions and the correct formulas for success.

Frog Heaven
A frog went to a fortuneteller and was told that he'd soon meet an attractive young woman who would get very close to him and who would have an intense desire to learn more about him. "Where will I meet her?" the frog asked excitedly. "On a blind date?"

"No," replied the fortuneteller, "in Biology class."

The Skinny on Skin
A junior high teacher was grading a science test at home that she had given to her class and was reading some of the results to her husband. The subject was the human body, and the first question was "Name one of the major functions of your skin."

One child had written, "To keep people who look at you from throwing up."

Wet States

A seventh-grade Science teacher had been enlightening his class about the solid, liquid, and gaseous states of matter. He asked, "In what states does water exist in nature?"

One fast-thinking student blurted out, "It's in all fifty, isn't it?"

Rest Home

In his Science test, sixth-grader Herschel answered a question about hibernation: "Into what state of inactivity do some animals with fur coats go during the winter months?"

Young Herschel wrote, "Florida."

Weird Science

When the Biology teacher asked Tommy to identify three character-istics of marine life, he answered, "Drilling, going on long hikes, and sleeping in tents."

What Are You?

The first-grade teacher was talking to her class about nature. She asked Donna in the third row, "Are you animal, vegetable, or mineral?"

"I'm not any of those," Donna replied quickly. "I'm a real live girl."

A Bright Idea

Teacher: Which is more important to us, the sun or the moon?
Student: The moon.
Teacher : Why?
Student: The moon gives us light at night when we need it, but the sun gives us light only in the daytime when we don't need it.

An Answer with Conviction

Biology teacher: Name something found in cells.
Student: Prisoners.

Don't Know Much about Biology

Teacher: What is a group of whales called? I'll give you a hint. It sounds like a device you use to listen to music.
Student: An iPod?
Teacher: Close. But what I'm thinking of is a little smaller.
Student: A Shuffle?

Here's Why

In Physics class, the professor was discussing a particularly complicated concept. A pre-medical student rudely interrupted, demanding, "Why do we have to learn all this stuff?"

"To save lives," the professor responded quickly and continued the lecture.

A few minutes later, the same student spoke up again. "So, how exactly does physics save lives?" he persisted.

"It keeps the idiots out of medical school," replied the professor.

The Creation

A student in a Science class wrote, "The universe is a giant orgasm" (instead of "organism").

At the end of the student's essay, the teacher commented, "Your answer gives new meaning to the Big Bang Theory."

The Body Eccentric

Here is a description of the human body, reputedly written by a Seattle student:

The human body is composed of three parts: the Brainium, the Borax, and the Abominable Cavity. The Brainium contains the brain. The Borax contains the lungs, the liver, and the living things. The Abominable Cavity contains the bowels, of which there are five: A, E, I, O, and U.

37

Doing the Numbers

I've never been good at math. I accepted it from a very early age.
My teacher would hand me a math test.
I'd just write on it, "I'm going to marry someone who can do this."
—RITA RUDNER

Math was my worst subject because I could never persuade the teacher
that my answers were meant ironically.
—CALVIN TRILLIN

They say you use only ten percent of your brain. What about the other ten?
—LARA BLISS

Teaching kids to count is fine, but teaching them what counts is best.
—BOB TALBERT

Math teachers are a good addition to our lives. They are benevolent rulers of their classrooms. They cut a fine figure and are always in their prime.

Math teachers are unfailingly rational, radical, acute, integral, and integrated—never average, derivative, indiscriminate, obtuse, or mean. They love to go off on tangents, but they always come up with the right angle. They treat you fair and square.

Math teachers help you to solve problems. They tell you to multiply and be fruitful. They teach you to divide and conquer. Their lessons on decimals are always to the point. And they realize that five out of four of us have difficulty with fractions.

Math teachers are as good as spectacles because they improve division. They make Geometry as easy as pi. They encourage us to revel in "Times Square." They deserve a comfortable retirement and enjoyable after-math.

"Addition is sum fun," declare math teachers sum merrily, "and fractions speak louder than words." They show us that there's safety in numbers. They teach us to make straight *As*—with a ruler. And they might even cosine a loan.

No wonder some of the cleverest teacher jokes are about math class:

Doing a Number on Recruiting
The Mathematics Department felt they weren't getting enough students registering as Math majors, so they made a commercial and aired it at prime time: 1 o'clock, 2 o'clock, 3 o'clock, 5 o'clock, 7 o'clock, and 11 o'clock.

Counting Sheep
"If there were a dozen sheep, and six of them jumped over the fence, how many would be left?" asked the Math teacher.

"None," answered Charlie.

"None, Charlie? I don't think you know your math."

"I don't think you know your sheep. When one jumps, they all follow!"

Sum Understanding
Teacher: If you received $10 from ten people, what would you get?
Student: A new bike.

What's Missing?
Teacher: Please recite the numbers of 1 to 10.
Student: 1, 2, 3, 4, 5, 6, 7, 8, 10.
Teacher: Didn't you forget something? What happened to 9?
Student: 7 8 9.

A Debatable Answer
Teacher: What is Forensics?
Student: Forensics is ten.
Monthly Allowance
Teacher: Which month has twenty-eight days?
Student: All of them.

Go Figure

Teacher: Ralph, if your father has $10 and you ask him for $6, how much would your father still have?

Ralph: $10.

Teacher: You don't know your math.

Ralph: You don't know my father!

Harebrained Math

Teacher: If I give you two rabbits and two more rabbits and then another two, how many rabbits will you have?

Student: Seven.

Teacher: Are you sure that the answer isn't six?"

Student: It's seven. I already have a rabbit at home.

Symbolic Logic

Reviewing math symbols, a teacher drew a greater-than and less-than symbol on the chalkboard and asked her second-graders, "Who knows what these mean?"

One boy's hand confidently shot up. "Fast forward and rewind!"

TV or Not TV

The math teacher saw that little Johnny wasn't paying attention in class. She called on him and asked, "Johnny, what are 2 and 4 and 28 and 44?"

Johnny quickly replied, "NBC, FOX, ESPN, and the Cartoon Network."

Clowning Around

Teacher: If I had seven oranges in one hand and eight oranges in the other, what would I have?

Class Clown: Big hands!

Halloween Geometry

Teacher: What do you get when you divide the circumference of a jack-o'-lantern by its diameter?

Student: Pumpkin pi.

The Bible Tells Me So

Mrs. Johnson, the elementary school Math teacher, was having children do problems on the blackboard that day. "Who would like to do the first problem, addition?"

No one raised their hand. She called on Jimmy, and with some help he finally got it right.

"Who would like to do the second problem, subtraction?'

Students hid their faces. She called on Mark, who laboriously solved the problem.

"Who would like to do the third problem, division?"

Now a low collective groan could be heard as everyone looked at nothing in particular. The teacher called on Suzy, who got it right

"Now, who would like to do the fourth problem, multiplication?"

Tim's hand shot up, surprising everyone in the room. Mrs. Johnson asked, "Why the enthusiasm, Tim?"

"Because God said to go forth and multiply!"

38

Hysterical History

*It would take us only one generation of forgetfulness
to put us back intellectually thousands of years.*
–DEAN TOFFLESON

*Not to know the events which happened before one was born,
that is to remain always a boy.*
–MARCUS TULLIUS CICERO

Whoso neglects learning in his youth loses the past and is dead for the future.
–EURIPIDES

Education is the transmission of civilization.–WILL DURANT

*I cannot understand why I flunked American History.
When I was young, there was so little of it.*
–GEORGE BURNS

History teachers make the past perfect and give us the present of the past. That past lengthens our lives in a way because for each person history is part of his story.

A Question of Greatness
Teacher: What do George Washington, Abraham Lincoln, and Martin Luther King Jr. have in common?
Student: They were all born on holidays.

Location, Location
Teacher: Where was the Declaration of Independence signed?
Student: At the bottom.

Hatchet Job

Teacher: After George Washington chopped down a cherry tree, he admitted it to his father. Why didn't his father punish him?

Student: Because Washington still had the axe in his hand.

In the Right

A fifth-grade teacher told her students that members of her profession in the 1800s dressed in ankle-length skirts and long-sleeved blouses, even in summertime. She went on to explain that such garb was necessary because teachers were not allowed to expose their arms or legs.

A boy piped up from the back of the room: "Oh no, that can't be true. The Constitution gave everyone the right to bare arms."

Lincoln Log

Student: Do you know why I'm smarter than Abraham Lincoln?

Teacher: No, why?

Student: Because I'm ten, and I can already recite The Gettysburg Address. President Lincoln had to wait until he was fifty.

History Lesson

Memorial Day was coming up, and the nursery school teacher took the opportunity to tell her class about patriotism. "We live in a great country," she said. "One of the things we should be happy about is that, in this country, we are all free."

One little boy came walking up to her from the back of the room. He stood with his hands on his hips and said "I'm not free!"

Taken aback by the boy's assertiveness, the teacher said, "Well, at your age I will admit that you are not allowed to do anything you want, but what I meant is that your family can do anything that is legal. Now, do you understand that you are free?"

"No—I'm not free!" the pupil said looking up defiantly, "I'm four!"

A Long Time Ago

Teacher: What happened in the year 1492?

Student: How should I know? I wasn't alive back then.

The Napoleonic Code

Teacher: Can you tell me the nationality of Napoleon?
Student: Course I can.
Teacher: That is correct.

Making History

The seventh-graders had been studying a unit about World War II and a test question was "What was the largest amphibious invasion of all time?"

Expecting to see "the D-Day invasion" as the answer, the teacher found, instead, on one paper, "Moses and the plague of frogs."

History Mystery

Mrs. Taylor asked her fifth grade History class, "When was Rome built?" and called on Timothy to answer first.

"Rome was built at night."

"At night? How ever did you get such an idea, Timothy?"

"Well, everyone knows Rome wasn't built in a day."

A Stock Answer

An American History teacher, lecturing the class on the Puritans, asked, "What sort of people were punished in the stocks?"

From the back of the room, little Melvin responded, "The small investor."

Lost in Translation

*I like a teacher who gives you something
to take home to think about besides homework.*
–LILY TOMLIN

What the Teacher Says	What the Teacher Means
Donald is a fount of endless energy.	This hyperactive student can't stay seated for five minutes.
Madison possesses an exuberant verbosity.	She's a motor mouth.
Fantastic imagination! Un-matched	He's one of the biggest liars I have ever met in his capacity for blending fact with fiction.
Margie exhibits a casual, relaxed attitude to school, indicating that high expectations don't intimidate her.	She hasn't done one assignment all term.
Jeff's athletic ability is marvelous. Superior hand-eye coordination.	He stung me with a rubber band from fifteen feet away.
Sally thrives on interaction with her peers.	She needs to stop socializing and start working.
Bert has a remarkable ability to gather needed information from his classmates.	He was caught cheating on a test.

What the Teacher Says	What the Teacher Means
Sarah throws herself into demonstrative public discussions.	Classroom lawyer. Why is it that every time I explain an assignment she stokes a class argument?
John enjoys the thrill of engaging in challenges with his peers.	He's a bully.
Cloe is an adventurous nature lover who rarely misses opportunities to explore the environment.	She was caught skipping school and fishing at the pond.
Unlike some students who hide their emotions, Travis is very expressive and open.	He must have written the *Whiner's Guide*.
Anna's intellectual and emotional progress would be enhanced through a year's repetition of her learning environment.	She is not ready for high school and should repeat the eighth grade.

40

More Teacher Tales

It is not knowledge, but the act of learning, not possession,
but the act of getting there, which grants the greatest enjoyment.
–CARL FRIEDRICH GAUSS

Genius In the Classroom

As a ten-year-old student, Carl Friedrich Gauss (1777–1855) was presented the following mathematical problem: What is the sum of the numbers from 1 to 100?

While his classmates were frantically calculating with paper and pencil, Gauss immediately envisioned that if he spread out the numbers 1 through 50 from left to right, and the numbers 51 through 100 from right to left directly below the 1–50 numbers, each combination would add up to 101 (1 + 100, 2 + 99, 3 + 98 and so on). Since there were fifty combinations, the answer would be 50 x 101 = 5050.

To the astonishment of everyone, including the teacher, young Carl not only reached the answer ahead of everyone else, but computed it entirely in his mind before writing it in on his slate. His teacher was so impressed that he invested his own money to purchase the best available textbook on arithmetic and gave it to young Gauss stating, "You are beyond me. I can teach you nothing more."

Carl Friedrich Gauss went on to become one of the greatest mathematicians in history, his theories still used today in the service of science. And he became a mathematics teacher to others, some of whom contributed their flashing insights to the field and left legacies of their own.

–Arthur Benjamin

Try, Try Again

A Middle East fable tells of a sparrow lying on its back in the middle of a road with its legs thrust up. Along comes a horseman who, seeing the sparrow, dismounts and asks, "Why are you lying here on your back in the middle of the road?"

"Because I have heard that the heavens will fall today."

"I see. And you think you can hold them up with those spindly legs of yours?"

And the bird answers: "One must do what one can."

Blinded by the Enlightenment

A monk once approached a venerable master with a request for mentoring in reaching the enlightened state. "If I study eight hours a day, four days a week, how long will it take me?" asked the student.

"Five years," answered the master.

That was too long for the impatient young monk, who tried again: "And if I studied sixteen hours, seven days a week?"

"In that case," responded the master, it will take ten years."

Moral: One who is in a hurry learns slowly.

A Graduate School Fable

One sunny day, a rabbit came out of her hole in the ground to enjoy the weather. The day was so nice that the rabbit became careless, so a fox sneaked up on her and caught her.

"I am going to eat you for lunch!" said the fox.

"Wait!" replied the rabbit, "You should wait a few days."

"Oh yeah? Why should I wait?"

"Well, I'm just finishing writing my PhD dissertation."

"Hah! That's a stupid excuse. What's the title of your thesis, anyway?"

"It's on 'The Superiority of Rabbits over Foxes and Wolves.'"

"Are you crazy? I should eat you up right now! Everybody knows that a fox will always defeat a rabbit!"

"Not really, not according to my research. If you like, you can come to my hole and read my thesis for yourself. If you're not convinced, you can go ahead and eat me for lunch."

"You really are crazy!" But, since the fox was curious and had nothing to lose, he disappeared into the rabbit's hole. The fox never came back out.

A few days later, the rabbit was again taking a break from her research and writing and, sure enough, a wolf came out of the bushes and grabbed her.

"Wait!" yelled the rabbit, "You can't eat me right now."

"And why might that be, you fuzzy appetizer?" asked the wolf.

"I'm almost finished writing my PhD dissertation on 'The Superiority of Rabbits over Foxes and Wolves.'"

The wolf laughed so hard that he almost lost his hold on the rabbit. "Maybe I shouldn't eat you. You really are sick in your head, and you might have something contagious," the wolf opined.

"Come read it for yourself. You can eat me after that if you disagree with my conclusions." So the wolf went to the rabbit's hole, and never came out again.

The rabbit finished writing her thesis and was out celebrating in the lettuce fields. Another rabbit came by and asked, "What's up? You seem very happy."

"Yep, I just finished writing my dissertation."

"Congratulations! What's it about?"

"It's titled 'The Superiority of Rabbits over Foxes and Wolves.'"

"Are you sure? That doesn't sound right."

"Oh yes, you should come over and read it for yourself."

So they went together to the rabbit's hole. As they entered, the friend saw the typical graduate student abode, chaotic and strewn with books and papers. The computer with the controversial dissertation was in one corner. On the right there was a pile of fox bones, on the left a pile of wolf bones, and in the middle sat a ginormous lion.

Moral: The title of your dissertation doesn't matter. The quality of the research doesn't matter. All that really matters is who your thesis adviser is.

A Teacher's Night Before Christmas

(with thanks to Clement Clark Moore)

'Twas the week before Christmas, and all through the school
Not a pupil was silent, no matter what rule.
The children were dressed up in whites and in reds
While vacation visions danced 'round in their heads.

The teacher, who'd taught in the classroom for years,
Had just settled down to work with her dears,
When out in the hall there arose such a clatter
Up sprang the kids to see what was the matter.

Away to the door they all flew like a flash.
The one who was leading went down with a crash.
Then what to their wondering eyes did they see
But a stately and shapely tall, green Christmas tree.

When the good teacher saw this, her heart swelled with joy.
She happily summoned each girl and each boy.
More rapid than coursers, the little ones came,
And the teacher smiled brightly and called them by name:

"Now Tommy! Now Sandy! Now Judy and Darrell!
Stop, Billy! Stop Suzie! Stop, Donny and Carol!
Now get to your places. Get away from the hall!
Now get away! Get away! Get away, all!"

As leaves that before the wild hurricane fly,
The pupils, pell-mell, started scurrying by.
They ran to the blackboard and skipped down the aisle.
Their faces were shining, and each had a smile.

First came a basket of popcorn to string.
Then came the Christmas tree—beautiful thing!
When they brought the tree in, there arose a great shout.
The pupils were merrily romping about.

The teacher and children with great gusts of glee
Festooned with bright lights the divine Christmas tree.
The colorful balls and the tinsel they hung.
The peppermint canes and the popcorn they strung.

When they placed the bright angel on top of the tree,
The school bell rang out, and the children were free.
Their shrill little voices soon faded away,
And peace was restored at the end of the day.

As she looked at the Christmas tree, glistening and tall,
The teacher called out, "Merry Christmas to all!"
And after the furor, the frenzy, the fuss,
We give every teacher a grade of A+!

A Teacher's Garden of Verses

I maintain, in truth,
That with a smile, we should instruct our youth,
Be very gentle when we have to blame,
And not put them in fear of virtue's name.
–MOLIERE

School Days

School days, school days,
Dear old golden rule days.
Readin' and 'ritin' and 'rithmetic,
Taught to the tune of the hickory stick.
You were my queen in calico.
I was your bashful barefoot beau,
And you wrote on my slate.
"I love you, so."
When we were a couple of kids.

Nothing to do, Nellie Darling,
Nothing to do, you say.
Let's take a trip on memory's ship
Back to the bygone days.
Sail to the old village school house,
Anchor outside the school door,
Look in and see
There's you and there's me,
A couple of kids once more.

–Will D. Cobb

Only the Brave

Only the brave. Only the brave should teach.
Only those who love the young should teach.
Teaching is a vocation.
It is as sacred as the priesthood;
As innate a desire, as inescapable as the genius
Which compels a great artist.
If he has not the concern for humanity,
The love of living creatures,
The vision of the priest and the artist,
He must not teach.

–Pearl Buck

Building the Future

A builder builded a temple,
He wrought it with grace and skill;
Pillars and groins and arches,
All fashioned to work his will.
Men said, when they saw its beauty,
"It shall never know decay;
Great is thy skill, O Builder!
Thy fame shall endure for aye."

A teacher builded a temple,
With loving and infinite care,
Planning each arch with patience,
Laying each stone with prayer.
None praised her unceasing efforts,
None knew of her wondrous plan,
For the temple the teacher builded,
Was unseen by the eyes of man.

Gone is the builder's temple,
Crumbled into dust;
Low lies each stately pillar
Food for consuming rust.
But the temple the teacher builded
Will last while the ages roll,
For that beautiful unseen temple
Was a child's immortal soul.

To a Special Teacher

With a special gift for learning
And a heart that deeply cares,
You add a lot of love and good
To everything you share,
And even though you mean a lot,
You'll never know how much,
Because you help to change the world
Through every life you touch.

You've sparked the creativity
In students you have taught,
And helped them strive for lofty goals
That simply can't be bought,
You are such a special teacher
That no words can truly tell
However much you're valued
For the work you do so well.

Whose Child Is This?

"Whose child is this?" I asked one day,
Seeing a little one out at play.
"Mine," said the parent with a tender smile,
"Mine to keep a little while,
To bathe his hands and comb his hair,
To tell him what he is to wear,
To set him on the path to good
And each day do the things he should."

"Whose child is this?" I asked one day,
Seeing the little one out at play.
"Mine," said the teacher with the same tender smile,
"Mine, to keep a little while,
To teach him how to be gentle and kind,
To train and direct his dear little mind,
To help him live by the Golden Rule
And get the best he can from school."

"Whose child is this?" I ask once more,
Just as the little one came through the door.
"Ours," the parent and teacher smiled
And each took the hand of the little child.
"Ours to love and train together;
Ours this blessed task forever."

43

Education Quotations

Humorists on Education

- Training is everything. The peach was once a bitter almond; cauliflower is nothing but cabbage with a college education.–*Mark Twain*

- A good education is the next best thing to a pushy mother. –*Charles M. Schulz*

- I was a substitute teacher for a couple of years, and it's a tough job. And apparently not cool to say, "You guys work on your math problems. If you have any questions, wake me up."–*Adam Gropman*

- My school was so tough that the school newspaper had an obituaries section.–*Norm Crosby*

- It was my SAT scores that led me into my present vocation in life, comedy–*Neil Simon*

- I read Shakespeare and the Bible and I can shoot dice. That's what I call a liberal education.–*Tallulah Bankhead*

- Nothing I learned in school prepared me for life at any level. My first book should have read, "See Dick balance his checkbook. See Jane leave an unhealthy relationship. Run, Jane, run!–*Kate Mason*

- College is supposed to prepare you for the real world, but if that's the case, they should have a class on standing in line. The post office line. The DMV line. Grocery store line. Unless Shakespeare's clever wordplay can help me cut in front of that mom and screaming baby at the market, he's of no use to me.–*Rosie Tran*

- Educational television should be absolutely forbidden. It can only lead to unreasonable expectations and eventual disappointment when your child discovers that the letters of the alphabet do not leap up out of books and dance around the room with royal-blue chickens. –*Fran Liebowitz*

- Smartness runs in my family. When I went to school, I was so smart my teacher was in my class for five years.–*Gracie Allen*

- I'll never forget my first day of school. My mom woke me up, got me dressed, made my bed, and fed me. Man, did the guys in the dorm tease me.–*Michael Aronin*

- In California, some high schools are requiring students to wear uniforms. They say uniforms create a safe, stable environment. You know, like the post office.–*Jay Leno*

- Schools: I got an *F* one time on a question that asked my opinion. –*Gallagher*

- You know how to tell if the teacher is hung over? Movie Day.–*Jay Mohr*

- One of the disadvantages of having children is that they eventually grow old enough to give you presents they make at school. –*Robert Byrne*

- Often, when I am reading a good book, I stop and thank my teacher. That is, I used to, until she got an unlisted number.–*Rita Rudner*

- It was different when we were kids. In second grade, a teacher came in and gave us all a lecture about not smoking, and then they sent us over to arts and crafts to make ashtrays for Mother's Day. –*Paul Clay*

- I had a teacher who was very rude. She said, "Remember, the sky's the limit." Sure, it sounds nice, but I had just told her I wanted to be an astronaut.–*Kellen Erskine*
- I dropped out of college after two years, and now I'm kicking myself because if I had played my cards just a little differently, I could have a community college diploma right now.–*Shmuel Breban*
- Never try to teach a pig to sing. It wastes your time and annoys the pig.–*Author Unknown*

But Seriously . . .

- It is easier to build strong children than to repair broken men. –*Frederick Douglass*
- Teaching, is not just a job. It is a human service, and it must be thought of as a mission.–*Ralph Tyler*
- Teaching people skills without giving them a vision for a better future, a vision based on common values, is only training.–*Nido Qubein*
- It is the mark of an educated mind to be able to entertain a thought without accepting it.–*Aristotle*
- Plants are shaped by cultivation and men by education. We are born weak, we need strength; we are born totally unprovided, we need aid; we are born stupid, we need judgment. Everything we do not have at our birth and which we need when we are grown is given us by education.–*Jean Jacques Rousseau*
- Learning is not attained by chance. It must be sought for with ardor and attended to with diligence.–*Abigail Adams*
- It is the universal condition of mankind to want to know.–*Hernan Cortes*
- Human history becomes more and more a race between education and catastrophe.–*H. G. Wells*
- There are three ingredients in the good life—learning, earning, and yearning.–*Christopher Morley*
- To me, education is the leading out of what is already in the pupil's soul.–*Muriel Spark*
- The pupil who is never required to do what he cannot do never does what he can do.–*John Stuart Mill*

- Be careful to leave your sons well instructed rather than rich, for the hopes of the instructed are better than the wealth of the ignorant.–*Epictetus*
- To teach is to learn twice.–*Joseph Joubert*
- If you would thoroughly know anything, teach it to others.–*Tryon Edwards*
- The object of education is to prepare the young to educate themselves throughout their lives.–*Robert Maynard Hutchins*
- The object of teaching a child is to enable him to get along without his teacher.–*Elbert Hubbard*
- The world can never be considered educated until we spend as much on books as we do on chewing gum.–*Elbert Hubbard*
- Learning makes a man fit company for himself.–*Thomas Fuller*
- What the pupils want to learn is as important as what the teachers want to teach.–*Lois E. LaBar*
- The important thing is not so much that every child should be taught, but that every child should be given the wish to learn. –*John Lubbock*
- Fortune favors the prepared mind.–*Peter Drucker*
- There is only one good, knowledge, and one evil, ignorance. –*Socrates*
- The man who can make hard things easy is the educator –*Ralph Waldo Emerson*
- We worry about what a child will be tomorrow, yet we forget that he or she is somebody today.–*Stacia Tauser*
- An educated man is one who can entertain a new idea, entertain another person, and entertain himself.–*Sydney J. Wood*
- The three Rs—reading, 'riting, and 'rithmetic—are no longer enough. We must add the three Cs–computing, critical thinking, and capacity for change.–*Fred Gluck*

44

A Teacher's Legacy

I touch the future. I teach.–CHRISTA McAULIFFE

Whoever teaches his son teaches not only his son
but his son's son, and so on to the end of generations.
–HEBREW PROVERB

The greatest use of a life is to spend it for something that will outlast it.
–WILLIAM JAMES

Most of us end up with no more than five or six people who remember us.
Teachers have thousands of people who remember them
for the rest of their lives.
–ANDY ROONEY

A teacher is one who, in his youth, admired teachers.
–H. L. MENCKEN

All one can really leave one's children is what's inside their heads.
Education, in other words, and not earthly possessions,
is the ultimate legacy, the only thing that cannot be taken away
–WEHRNER VON BRAUN

When you speak, your words echo across the room.
When you teach, your words echo across the ages.
–RICHARD LEDERER

Teacher to Teacher

A woman attended her twentieth high school reunion, where she encountered her freshman year Art teacher. She told him that she had decided to go to college as a result of his inspiration and that she was now an Art professor at a large state university.

At the end of the evening's festivities, the teacher searched out his former student, shook her hand, and said, "Thank you for saying those nice things about my teaching. You've made my day."

"You're welcome," said the woman as she hugged him. "But let me thank you, sir. You've made my life."

The Awakening

I can still remember it like it was yesterday. I was a college freshman and had stayed up most of the previous night laughing and talking with friends. Now just before my first class of the day, my eyelids were feeling heavier and heavier, and my head was drifting down to my desk to make my textbook a pillow. A few minutes nap time before class couldn't hurt, I thought.

BOOM! My head jerked up and my eyes snapped open wider than saucers. I looked around with my heart pounding trying to locate the source of the noise. My young professor was looking back at me with a mischievous, boyish grin on his face. He had intentionally dropped on the lectern the stack of textbooks he was carrying. "Good morning!" he said still smiling. "I am glad to see everyone is awake. Now let's get started."

For the next hour I wasn't sleepy at all. It wasn't from the shock of my professor's textbook alarm clock either. It was, instead, from the fascinating discussion he led. With knowledge and good humor he made the material come alive. His insights were full of wisdom and loving kindness, and the enthusiasm and joy that he taught with were contagious. I left the classroom not only wide awake, but a little smarter and a little better.

That day I learned something far more important than not sleeping in class. I learned that if you are going to do something in this life, do it well, do it with joy, and make it an expression of your love. What a glorious place this would be if all of us did our work joyously and well. What a beautiful world we could create if every doctor, teacher, musician, preacher, cook, mechanic, waitress, businessman, fisherman, poet, miner, farmer, and laborer made their work an expression of their love.

Don't sleepwalk your way through life then. Wake up! Let your love fill your work and God's love fill your soul. Life is too short not to live it well.

–Joseph J. Mazzella

The End?

The teacher looked ahead with misgivings but with hope.
Would the way be smooth or rough?
Would it end in success or failure?
And she stood and looked and wondered.
And a voice said: "There will be no end."

And the teacher smiled and said:
"I know it will end. I may teach one year, two years,
Or possibly many years,
But this I know: Someday it will end."
And the teacher went forth to teach.

And many gathered around her,
And they all had need to learn.
And the teacher looked into their eyes
And desired to fill their needs.
And she taught them with mind and heart and voice—
A mind filled with knowledge,
A voice speaking wisdom,
And a heart overflowing with love.

Then life changed, and the teacher taught no more.
No more did eager students gather around her.
"It has ended," said the teacher, continuing on the road of life.
"This is the end of my teaching."

And she believed this until . . .
A doctor stood and said, "I am here because this teacher taught me."
A lawyer stood and said, "I am here because this teacher taught me."
An astronaut stood and said, "I am here because this teacher taught me."
An engineer stood and said, "I am here because this teacher taught me."
A teacher stood and said, "I am here because this teacher taught me."

And the teacher looked ahead of those whom she had taught

And saw the continued steps of progress before each one.
And joy filled the teacher's heart, and she said,
"This is not the end. There is no end to my teachings."